ARTHUR PHILLIP

What makes a nation's pillars high
    And its foundations strong?
What makes it mighty to defy
    The foes that round it throng?

It is not gold. Its kingdoms grand
    Go down in battle shock;
Its shafts are laid on sinking sand,
    Not on abiding rock.

Is it the sword? Ask the red dust
    Of empires passed away;
The blood has turned their stones to rust,
    Their glory to decay.

And is it pride? Ah, that bright crown
    Has seemed to nations sweet;
But God has struck its lustre down
    In ashes at His feet.

Not gold but only men can make
    A people great and strong;
Men who for truth and honour's sake
    Stand fast and suffer long.

Brave men who work while others sleep,
    Who dare while others fly –
They build a nation's pillars deep
    And lift them to the sky.

                                        Emerson

Arthur Phillip

Thea Stanley Hughes

ISBN 0 908076 15 0

Printed in Australia by STAR PRINTERY PTY. LTD.
21 Coulson Street, Erskineville, N.S.W. 2042. Telephone: 516 2100

Typeset by TYPESETTING BY TELEPHONE ☎ (02) 90 4034

FOREWORD

In presenting this study of Arthur Phillip, Thea Stanley Hughes is expressing her deep conviction that the life and achievements of Australia's founding governor need to be told once more for the rising generations in this country. The author has fulfilled her purposes with lucidity and brevity. In a brief space, she has managed to convey the essentials of the British background, the voyage to Botany Bay and the early, testing period of settlement. The reader is made an immediate spectator and, at the same time, is constantly reminded of the long-term importance of these events of the late eighteenth century for the present circumstances of Australia.

Kenneth J. Cable
President, Royal Australian Historical Society, 1977-82.
Associate Professor in History, University of Sydney

There is a tide in the affairs of men,
Which, taken at the flood, leads on to fortune;
Omitted, all the voyage of their life
Is bound in shallows and in miseries:
And we must take the current when it serves,
Or lose our ventures.

Shakespeare

Contents

LIST OF ILLUSTRATIONS

BIBLIOGRAPHY

Books written by those taking part in the first five years.

Phillip, Arthur, *Voyage to Botany Bay.*
Collins, David, *An Account of the British Colony in N.S.W.*
Hunter, John, *Historical Journal of the Transactions at Port Jackson and Norfolk Island.*
Tench, Watkin, *Sydney's First Four Years.*
White, John, *Journal of a Voyage to N.S.W.*

Others

Carter, Theo, *In A Strange Land – Pioneers of Australia.*
Clark, C.M.H. and Pryor, L.J., *Select Documents in Australia.*
Cobley, John, *Sydney Cove 1788, Sydney Cove, 1789-1790, Sydney Cove, 1791-1792.*
Eldershaw, M. Barnard, *Phillip of Australia.*
Encyclopedia Britannica.
Gordon, Mona, *The Mystery of La Perouse.*
Historical Records of Australia, Series 1, vol. 1.
Lee, Sidney, *Dictionary of National Biography.*
Mackaness, George, *Admiral Arthur Phillip; Banks and Phillip.*
Rutter, O, *First Fleet.*
Summit Publications (Hamlyn), *Complete History of Australia.*

Introduction

In a broadcast given in 1982, it was said that the Australian people seem to think about Arthur Phillip only about the end of January. At the same time, random interviews, asking people what Australia Day meant to them, were broadcast. The answers made it quite clear that there are many adults who do not know anything about Arthur Phillip. In answer to the question concerning what Australia Day was about, quite a number said, "Captain Cook landed". This is a bit confusing but not as confusing as an answer given about sixty years ago. In the Royal Australian Historical Society Journal, 1918, somebody is quoted as saying that an intelligent man was asked what happened on the 26th January, 1788 and that the answer was, "Captain Cook landed at Circular Quay in a ship called *La Perouse*".

As much attention has been given to the general ignorance about Arthur Phillip, it should also be mentioned that, at some Australian universities, there is, in the last few years, an increasing interest in Australian history. If people in general were to make an effort to be more aware of the sort of man the first Governor was, surely the celebration of Australia Day would become more meaningful.

The future of a nation depends partly on which ideas and examples are brought forward to be used — with the new ones — in the preparation for the future. In a recent letter to the editor of a daily newspaper, the writer said that in no other country would such a founder be so unrevered. Is it insensitivity that is disconnecting us from what is valuable and bracing in our past?

As members of a nation, we need to have historical records of the events surrounding its foundation and we are fortunate to have very good ones. It is now possible to obtain books containing the journals written by Captain John Hunter, Judge-Advocate* David Collins, Surgeon John White, Captain Watkin Tench and Arthur Phillip himself, as they were taking part in the first five years of the first settlement.

Amongst writers, there are those who have respect for individuality and for truth but there are those who fall into a certain highly profitable and attractive temptation. It is the temptation to add new bits of 'information' either by plain statement or by the more cunning way of suggestion. It is interesting that it is quite fashionable to add a new bit of 'information' which was not mentioned either by the person's friends or enemies when he was alive. It is, at present, very much the fashion to use the printed word to belittle the great by making out that they would have done or felt as the majority would have done or felt in similar circumstances. It is no wonder this is done so frequently, as so many ideas we have been persuaded to believe add up to the belief that one man is as good as another.

So, perhaps, it is no wonder that Arthur Phillip is so little known, though he is really so closely related to millions of people who are benefiting not only from what he did but from the way he did it.

One would not know anything much about him by learning that he became Governor of a prison settlement and ruler (without council, committee or parliament) of a vast area – more than twice as large as England, Scotland, Ireland, Wales, France, Italy, West Germany, Austria, Belgium, Holland, Poland, Rumania, Hungary, Greece, Denmark, Czechoslovakia, Switzerland, Sweden, Finland, Portugal and Spain combined!

Others could have taken his titles and produced very different results. In fact, others had taken control of such settlements that did work through cruelties, rebellion and confused purposes to final disaster. We can say "no wonder" to all this sort of prelude to disaster when we get a feeling for the kind of forces that would be clashing against each other in prison settlements in strange lands.

The key to the writing and the reading of this book is the thought that the most important question – for anyone who is interested in results or possible results of an action – is not **what** is being done but **who** is doing it.

Thinking about this idea helps a person to see why so many schemes have no real value for the future. If there is to be value for the future, the person responsible for the founding of the thing has to have something in him that makes it possible for the thing to go through those transformations that are called for by the spirit of the times.

Two people can do the same thing or say the same words and get two extremely different results because it is what is in the person that goes on flowing secretly out into the world through the work or through the words.

In this case, this means, of course, that the most important consideration for us is not that the first settlement was a convict settlement. It was, but we can be helped to see how unimportant that is when we can see that there are many people walking round today who have done much more harm to the bodies and minds of their fellow human beings than was ever done by some of the convicts. For us, the important consideration is not that it was a convict settlement but that Arthur Phillip was the one called upon to conduct this most unusual experiment. The big question is what sort of a man was Arthur Phillip.

*David Collins is generally referred to as Judge-Advocate but actually he was Deputy-Judge-Advocate. In 1809, Ellis Bent, a trained lawyer, was appointed the first official Judge-Advocate.

A man's life is what his thoughts make of it.

Marcus Aurelius

ARTHUR PHILLIP ESQ
Captain General and Commander-in-Chief
From the original portrait painted by F. Wheatley
By kind permission of the Mitchell Library, Sydney

Destiny Calling

In the spring of 1787, a strange scene was being enacted on the southern shores of England. The people on the shore near Portsmouth would have seen eleven ships lying at anchor nearby. From March till May, they could have watched much activity – men bringing many loads to the waterfront, getting them onto boats and barges, taking them out to the side of the ships and then hoisting them, by means of windlasses, onto the decks to be stowed away. They could have watched the activity on the roads – horses and horse-drawn coaches arriving with crew, officers and sea-captains and open wagons rattling along full of men and women obviously being brought to the ships from the prisons. They could have watched the prisoners being taken by little boats to the ships.

On the 7th May, the people on the shore may have seen a man arriving by himself. He was a quiet, unobtrusive sort of man and not well known. So, they may not have guessed that he was the Commander-in-Chief of this fleet and of the whole expedition and experiment. He was not young, not tall, not commanding-looking, not robust and, indeed, far from well. Judging too quickly, it would have been easy to think that he did not have much in his favour while, actually, he had a great deal but it was hidden within him. So, those who could have been standing close to him, as he was stepping into the rowing boat to be taken to his ship, would never have realized what qualities were living in him to make him able to cope with anything that would face him.

Nobody would have known, and few know now, that on embarking, he made the resolution not to use his authority for any personal ends. As he stood on the deck of the *Sirius* – the flag-ship of this very special fleet – he was looking back at the England whose shores he had helped to guard with his life for so many years and he could reasonably have thought that it could be the last time he would see his beloved native land.

PREPARATION

This man, Arthur Phillip, was born in London of an English mother and a German father. His father had come from Frankfurt to London, had taken up the teaching of languages and had married a widow. Her previous husband, a relation of Lord Pembroke of the British Navy, had died in a war between Spain and Britain.

His mother's previous marriage had a great bearing on the course of this child's life, as it would seem it secured him admission to the school that formed the basis for his career as a seafaring man. The child must have been fed with exciting stories told by sailors and traders – stories of discovery of a new world that needed brave men.

Up to the age of twelve, he was educated by his father and then was sent to school at Greenwich, a school for the sons of naval men who had been killed or drowned in service at sea. At this school, the arrangement was the same for all the boys. They had three years' schooling and then went for five years on Merchant ships to learn the different skills connected with the seafaring life. They were taken on for further instruction and supervision by the master of a ship and they had to account to him for their work and conduct during those five years.

It is interesting that both Phillip and James Cook were exceptions to the rule, as they were both released from their bond earlier than usual and joined the Navy.

During Phillip's two years in the Merchant Service, his ship was trading between England and Greenland, so, he got to know the North Atlantic Ocean and proved that he was able to cope with the bitter winds and hard work on very poor rations.

A year after he joined the Navy, war broke out once again. This was the Seven Years' War between Britain and France, in which Cook was also engaged. They also served in other parts of the world, Phillip in the Mediterranean and the West Indies and Cook in Canada.

14

GAINING AGRICULTURAL EXPERIENCE

The Seven Years' War ended in 1763 and Phillip, now a lieutenant and twenty-five years old, was placed on the Reserve List of the Navy on half pay, which meant that he could be recalled at any moment to take up duty again.

Shortly afterwards, he married and this gave him an opportunity that had important results for the world. This marriage, as well as his father's, provided opportunities that were vital for him who was to be chosen for a certain unusual task. He spent some years in the south of England where he was fully occupied managing the estate that had come to him through the marriage and gaining experience in agricultural work and in administration of county affairs – working with groups of people in less fortunate positions. After six years, his marriage, through a mutually arranged agreement, came to an end.

PORTUGUESE ASSOCIATION

When war broke out between Spain and Portugal in 1774, Phillip requested permission from the Admiralty to join Britain's ally, Portugal, and serve in the Portuguese Navy. He showed early in his service with the Portuguese that he possessed extraordinary initiative, which came to light when he was in command of a converted merchantman. It had a cargo of four hundred criminals en route to Brazil. During this voyage an epidemic broke out on board, leaving him without sufficient men to man the ship. He quickly solved this problem by calling up the most energetic of the convicts and explaining the situation to them. He promised them that, if they would sail the ship and perform other duties appointed to them, he would speak on their behalf when he returned to Lisbon. The prisoners agreed to this and for their co-operation they were later rewarded with emancipation and small grants of land.

In 1778, when France again declared war on Britain, Phillip returned to the British Navy. Though the Portuguese were sorry to see him go, they admired him for his decision. That his association with his Commanding Officer, the Marquis da

Lavradio, was a mutually satisfying one is brought to our notice in the quote given on the inside of the front cover.

In 1781, he was promoted to the rank of post-captain and appointed to the *Europe*. He saw action in 1782 and in 1783 and sailed with reinforcements to the East Indies. However, negotiations put an end to the war and he was recalled to England. On the way back – because of a gale – he put into the harbour of Rio de Janeiro, making the acquaintance of the local officials there. This acquaintance would be renewed at a future time. In 1784, he again went on the Reserve List, on half pay. During the next two years, he did some surveying work for the Admiralty. By this time, he was forty-eight years of age. He had been through many nerve-racking and health-destroying experiences since he was fifteen years old.

ENGLAND BUSY

Before thinking about the life of this man from this time onwards, let us think about what had been happening on the land in England while he had been spending so much time on the sea.

The vast majority of people before the eighteenth century lived in villages, tilling the soil or working at many different handcrafts, making useful, beautiful and necessary things or in coastal townships, where fishing was added to all the rest. All goods were taken to local markets to be sold and bought.

There was quietness and the busyness was without frantic rush and fierce competition. There were no aeroplanes, no cars, no trucks, no trains and no telephones. The main sounds to be heard in the by-ways were human voices, the clip-clop of the horses' hooves, the live sounds of the animals in the fields and the twittering of the birds in the hedges. There the rain fell frequently and gently in contrast to the weather in tropical countries where people would experience violent storms and floods.

DISTANT RUMBLINGS

Science, industry and geographical discovery were being interwoven. Out of this, there would come many benefits but also many evils. Benefits showed themselves at a later time, while the more obvious evils worked themselves into the situation quickly. Crime increased and the legal system was such that it only made the situation worse.

This was to become apparent towards the end of the century when transportation of prisoners to America was stopped and the few prisons became so overcrowded that something had to be done.

For well over fifty years, transportation of prisoners had been accepted and carried out. This meant that the prison situation had been periodically relieved though not improved. The law meted out the same punishment – death or transportation – for petty thefts as for murder and for other crimes by which one person would do serious physical harm to another.

THE GOVERNMENT MOVES

As early as 1779, a Committee of the House of Commons was convened to look into the whole question of transportation. It was at this meeting that Sir Joseph Banks suggested Botany Bay.

During a time of parliamentary questioning in 1785, Sir Joseph Banks said, "Botany Bay is the only part of this Country which I have visited and I am confident that it is in every respect adapted to the purpose." (*First Fleet* by O. Rutter, pp 50–154.)

Several other suggestions were also made and some of them tried but, at the beginning of 1786, the Government was still undecided.

So it was not until August 1786 that a definite move was made. This move became the concern of two other government departments, the Treasury and the Admiralty.

The plan was to establish a prison settlement at Botany Bay. There would be over seven hundred and fifty prisoners on five transport ships accompanied by three storeships and two naval ships. There would be a further seven to eight hundred people in the expedition made up of the crews of the ships, the marines and other personnel such as doctors, a judge-advocate and a minister of religion.

So it was that, at the end of this year 1786, the Royal Navy advertised for the ships required and the Home Office chose the man who was to be in charge of the expedition.

PHILLIP RECEIVES THE APPOINTMENT

Somehow, though this man was not known to him, Lord Sydney, the Secretary of State for the Home Office, who was responsible for prisons and colonies, appointed Captain Arthur Phillip R.N. to this task.

There is no record giving certainty about who actually suggested Phillip but it is surmised generally that the man who made the vital connection between Lord Sydney and Phillip was Sir George Rose, who was the Secretary to the Treasury when Pitt was Prime Minister. The fact that Phillip was to name the second settlement he established Rose Hill, is considered as support for the probability that Rose was the one. Many a conversation never mentioned in print or word plays a vital part in the course of events that influences millions of people for better or for worse. If there was a conversation between Lord Sydney and Sir George Rose about Arthur Phillip, it played a vital part in the history of the Pacific.

The connection between Sir George Rose and Captain Arthur Phillip was made after Phillip was on the Reserve List from the Navy, had married and had settled on the land. He had become a neighbour of Sir George Rose. In those days, the owners of estates took part in the administration of county affairs. So, Rose would almost certainly have come to know Phillip not only in relation to his work on the land but also in relation to his work with people in less fortunate circumstances.

In whatever way this choice came about, it certainly was not through the Admiralty. This becomes quite clear in a quotation by Rusden given in the *Dictionary of National Biography*. "I cannot say", wrote Lord Howe of the Admiralty to Lord Sydney, "the little knowledge I have of Captain Arthur Phillip would have led me to select him for service of this nature". It also seems that the Navy in those days was not anxious to be publicly associated with this penal settlement, as Sir Charles Middleton refers to the expedition as "this disagreeable and troublesome business". In *A Complete History of Australia* (a Summit Books publication by Hamlyn) we find the statement, "his selection was criticised in some quarters, but in the event it would have been hard to find a better choice."

THE IMPORTANCE OF THE BEGINNING

The wisdom of the choice showed up even before the departure of the expedition from England. We tend to think of Phillip only as Governor for five years of the part of the continent that was later to be called Australia by Matthew Flinders. In a certain sense, his greatest task confronted him before he set sail. If we look far enough into the future to the results of any necessary venture, we can see that the ultimate results depend on what is in the mind and heart of the person responsible for the venture. There is no possibility of a good result unless there is the capacity for sacrifice, strength of will and conviction at the beginning. It is obvious that Phillip's whole life was filled with feeling for the future and with fearless resolution.

COMMISSION

Though the Government had been very slow in coming to the decision to transport prisoners to Botany Bay, once the decision was made, it was certainly in a hurry to get the deed done.

Phillip was handed the first commission on the 12th October 1786. This commission was obviously drawn up in a hurry, for it consisted of only one page and suggested that the expedition sail in December. It seems as if the Government's concern was to get rid of prisoners as soon as possible. The Government had other pressing problems that must have seemed more important to everyone except to the one who had decided to put everything that he had into this experiment. He had the capacity to hold onto the hope in spite of the fact that he seemed to be the only one who visualized the potential. As the story unfolds, the reader will see that the hopelessness from which so many people were to suffer was quite understandable.

Captain Arthur Phillip had been given command of the prisoners or convicts and the personnel of the naval ships, the *Sirius* and *Supply*. He did not have command over the marines or over the crews of the storeships or transports. He had been given the task of setting up the administration of the settlement that would lay the foundations that would be built upon for years to come.

WHAT WERE SOME OF THE TRIALS?

It was not long before Phillip had worked out his plans. Before he left, he had the commission re-written. By the time his suggestions were incorporated, it consisted of fourteen pages. He had in mind that whatever was not thought of or left behind would not be able to be obtained for at least eighteen months. He also saw that a great deal more had to be done before leaving than was mentioned by the Government. This meant the departure month was not December but the following May.

His first despatch to Lord Sydney started in the following way,"By my arriving at the settlement two or three months before the transports many and very great advantages would be gained. Huts would be ready to receive those convicts who were sick and they would find vegetables."(*First Fleet* by O. Rutter, pp 50 – 154)

It becomes obvious from his journals that, in his mind, it was of the greatest importance that he should be able to go ahead of the rest of the fleet. It must have been a shock to him that this suggestion was not considered.

Another thing of importance to him was that some free settlers should be included in the personnel of the experiment. Nothing was done about this.

He felt he should have information about the crimes of the convicts and also about their characters and their work capacities. This information was not supplied. It seems incredible that any man should be expected to have about 750 men and women in his charge knowing practically nothing about them – not knowing, for instance, which ones were seasoned criminals and which had committed petty thefts. There could have been some who had only stolen something needed to save the life of a sick child. Phillip was also told that he would have the custody of "ideots and lunaticks". One presumes he had to find out for himself who they were.

He asked that the tools and implements, all of which would be essential, should be of good quality. He was to find out that they were of very poor quality, did not last long and made the difficult work more difficult for people who were, on the whole, weak.

He pointed out the need for convicts who had some experience of farming, husbandry, carpentry, brick-making, brick-laying, gardening and other skills. He also pointed out the need for people who could oversee the work of the convicts and direct them in whatever they had to do. This was ignored.

He also requested that convicts were selected who were considered free of venereal complaints. No reassurance was given to him on this matter.

He had in mind to work towards building up the livestock. He was thwarted in achieving this because of not having people who could look after them, as well as having the difficulties of being in a country without knowing the grasses or the weather or the seasons. One cannot help thinking about what a difference it would have made to the lives of everyone if he had been given complete control of the preparation for this experiment. On the other hand, it must be remembered that his abilities for this work were not known to those in the political field. In spite of all the ignoring of his requests, he took a passionate sort of interest in attending to the many details left to his judgement – always with the thought of the welfare of everybody concerned.

1787

The transports, which had been loaded with convicts in different parts of England, were instructed to meet near Portsmouth in March 1787. Phillip had, from this time, the care of these people. After inspecting the ships, he wrote to Lord Sydney pointing out the need for another transport ship as the convicts were too crowded for such a long journey. This he was given. When the Surgeon, John White, reported that convicts on one of the transports had become ill because of the vermin on the ship, Phillip again wrote to the Home Office asking for the means for off-loading the people while the ships were scoured and done over with oil of tar, a strong disinfectant. This was granted. The ship was cleaned, the convicts were brought back on board and soon recovered from the illness. His care for the health of the convicts was very unusual in the transportation business.

So it was that from the 12th October till the time of sailing, Phillip was continually supervising, organizing and making sure of every detail possible. He must have suffered disappointment and frustration at the realization that there was no real co-operation for him or respect for his ideas of what would come out of the experiment.

Instead of being discontented, critical or angry about it, he proved himself capable of acceptance of what he could not change after he had done all in his power to change it. In all his actions he was particularly free from any kind of retaliation and was prepared to do all he could with what he had and never lost sight of the purpose for which he was working from the beginning.

In thinking about all this work being done, it must be remembered that it is always more difficult to do a thing for the first time. Captain Arthur Phillip was now responsible for supervising the transport of passengers from England to Australia for the first time. He was also about to be the first Governor in the country that became Australia.

AUSTRALIA WAITING

Quietly and busily the water of a little stream was wending its way through thick bushland on the eastern side of the continent to which these people were being sent. It was keeping on pouring its life into a harbour whose waters were, in turn, flowing into an ocean of some 80,000,000 square miles (about 200,000,000 square kilometres) stretching from Antarctica to the Bering Straits and from Africa to America.

At the beginning of the year 1788, this stream was soon to become the centre of an unusual scene. The newcomers would have to play their part without knowing that, behind the edge of the bushland, there were thousands of square miles of completely uncultivated land in which many strange, wild creatures were at home. They would have to start without knowing whether the natives would be friendly or hostile and without knowing what they held sacred. For instance, they would not know that these native people held in remembrance something that had been practically blotted out of the remembrance of civilized people. The natives held in reverence the presence of the unseen spirits and were not afraid to recognize the presence of evil spirits as well as the presence of the good.

While this voyage was taking place, as for thousands of years before, the eucalypt trees were filling the air with the pungency of their health-giving, volatile oils. At night, one of the most haunting of strange bird-calls, the call of the mopoke owl, was often sounding in the silence. The dawn would frequently be greeted with the loud bursts of the cheerful sound from the kookaburras. The sea was continuously beating against the rocks on the rugged shore-line or surging onto many miles of white or yellow sands. Over this undivided, unharmed but unhelped land – the last to be entrusted to civilized men – the starry worlds were still sending down their gentle but sustaining influence, as they had done for countless centuries.

Although many ships had from time to time plied these southern seas since the 15th century, this eastern coast of the largest island in the world remained a secret until, in 1770,

Captain James Cook discovered, charted and named it and so made it possible for other people to find it. It was to be another eighteen years before Captain Arthur Phillip arrived there. So, in 1788, the destinies of Cook, Phillip, Britain and Australia were brought into close association. It was at this time, too, that the little stream mentioned earlier became vitally important in the history of the New World.

Voyage

At 6 o'clock in the morning of the 13th May, 1787, Captain Arthur Phillip gave the order for the fleet to move from where it had been anchored for so long. As a naval ship had arrived to escort the fleet for 300 miles (482km), there were 12 ships accompanied by a fresh wind blowing from the right quarter, sailing – with the *Sirius* in the lead – down the Channel towards the Atlantic Ocean.

That he must have felt some relief that they had, at last, got away can be seen in his last despatch when he writes, "All our difficulties are ended". For seven months he had been planning, supervising and waiting to get away. He had had to cope with many petty concerns in relationship with politicians who had no real interest in what he was taking on.

As soon as possible after leaving, he suggested that the irons, with which most of the male convicts were shackled, be removed so that they could move around more easily during the day, be more able to keep themselves clean and take their clothes off at night. This, of course, made it easier for those who wanted to take advantage of his consideration. Even before the escort ship had departed, a plot to mutiny and take over one of the transport ships had been foiled. Phillip directed that the two ringleaders be transferred to his ship and, after having seen that they had been given a punishment that was for those days lenient, he sent them to another ship.

It was not long after weighing anchor that Phillip had made it known that the ships were to keep together. He established day and night signals, in order to regulate the speed and so keep them together. Each evening he pulled in his sails and carried a light on his maintop as a guide.

When it was time for the escort to leave, the weather was so rough that it was considered to be too dangerous for a boat to collect the last minute letters to England from the personnel of the other ships. Phillip writes that he had had great difficulty in writing his despatches. This was about two weeks after they had left England. Then, when the escort ship had received his despatches and turned for home, a salute was given and the eleven ships went on in the rough Atlantic weather into the unknown.

The next week must have been a time when Phillip would be keeping close watch on the behaviour of the convicts and the rest of the personnel. From all accounts, it is obvious that he wished to make the journey as good as possible for all concerned but he was to find that there were those amongst the convicts who would not respond to his consideration for them.

TENERIFFE

So that he could get fresh food and water, he decided to put in at Teneriffe. He had wanted to stay only a short time there but the means of getting the water to the ships was so slow that he had to stay for a week. The water was brought by means of pipes to the water's edge, then it had to be put into casks, which had been brought from the ships to the shore in small boats, taken back to the ships and hoisted on board. While in port, everyone had a good ration of "fresh meat, soft bread and vegetables daily".

In thinking about this voyage, it must be remembered that many convicts were in a poor state of health, some in advanced stages of disease. Some had died on board ship before the fleet set off. They were of all ages, ranging from children to one of eighty-nine years of age. However, their treatment under Phillip helped and from this port he wrote, "By the inclosed list your Lordship will see that the convicts are not so sickly as when we sailed." George Mackaness in his book *Admiral Arthur Phillip* makes the following assessment, "Phillip devoted careful and unremitting attention to the personal hygiene of his human cargo, and to the sanitation of his vessels."

RIO DE JANEIRO

The next port of call was Rio de Janeiro and the journey to it lasted for about seven weeks. On this part of the voyage, there was some bad weather. After this was over, Surgeon John White went round the ships and, considering the dampness, was surprised to find the people in "so good a state of health".

While at this port, Phillip and his officers were treated with much ceremony. During the month they stayed there, all the transports, which were by this time alive with vermin, were thoroughly cleaned and disinfected. The ships were caulked and the sails attended to. Again everybody had good rations of meat, rice and fresh vegetables. In a despatch written in Rio by Phillip to his friend Evan Nepean of the Home Office he writes, "With respect to the convicts they have all been allowed the liberty of the deck in the day and many of them during the night which has kept them much healthier than could have been expected." Ships were watered, stores taken on board and many varieties of seed, including orange seeds, were also bought.

CAPE TOWN

It was in the beginning of September that they set sail on the 4,000 mile (6437km) stretch to Cape Town. This stretch was to take nearly nine weeks. It appears to have been an uneventful time with the only outstanding incident being that a convict fell overboard and, in spite of all efforts, was drowned.

Cape Town was to be their last port of call before they arrived at their destination. A month was spent here taking on animals of different kinds and as much of everything that could be fitted on. Phillip had difficulty in obtaining flour and some other things, as there had been a drought just prior to their arrival.

It is in a letter written from this port that we can learn more about the leader of this expedition. Lieutenant Clark, a marine officer, wrote in a letter to a friend, Lieutenant Kempster, "Never were prisoners so taken care of than they have been by the Commodore since his first taking charge of them." After telling his friend about the liberal rations the marines and convicts received in ports he adds, "You will say not bad allowance for convicts . . . They have never before been treated more like children than prisoners." (Mitchell Library MMS) In another letter written by a convict to a "female friend in London" we can read, "It would not be doing justice to Governor Phillip's humanity, lenity and attentive regards to our health and happiness was I not to mention particularly the manner in which he treated us . . . allowing us every indulgence which prudence and discretion in our present situation would authorize."

The Judge-Advocate, David Collins must have been expressing the general feeling when, in November 1787, he said, "If ever we might enjoy the commerce of the world, was doubtful and uncertain . . . . All communications with family and friends now cut off, we were leaving the world behind us, to enter on a state unknown."

How long? That was the question now as the water supply had to last till they reached their destination. It was not long after leaving the Cape that everyone was rationed to three pints a day.

Still anxious to make what little preparation he could still make for his people, the last and only line of action left to him was to take the smaller naval ship, which he thought would be faster, and go ahead. About a week after leaving Cape Town, he let his officers know of his plan to transfer his pennant to the *Supply*, leaving Captain Hunter as Captain of the *Sirius* and in charge of those ships that did not sail with him, and he would take three of the fastest transports and some chosen convicts. Having made the necessary adjustments and arrangements, he, with the three transports, put upon all sail and, for the first time, the fleet broke up.

BOTANY BAY. *SIRIUS* AND CONVOY GOING IN. 21st January 1788.
By Lieutenant William Bradley. By kind permission of the Mitchell Library, Sydney

1788

After holding on to the hope that he would get there in time to make some preparations, he discovered that the *Supply* was not able to sail at any speed through the rough seas they encountered. He was to have the same experience as Captain Cook had had. They both found that ships that appeared satisfactory for the job in port were inadequate on the high seas. Then, after Phillip had sighted the southern part of the east coast of N.S.W., contrary winds caused another delay and it was a further two weeks before he finally reached Botany Bay.

It must be remembered that in those days there were no means of communication once ships were out of sight of each other. So, we can imagine the shock Phillip must have experienced after arriving at his destination on the 18th January, 1788 to see the three transports that left with him arrive the next day and the rest of the fleet on the morning of the following day. After about eight weeks' sailing, he had only a matter of hours to make preparations.

Original Gesture

In spite of the fact that their first sight of Botany Bay showed natives shouting and brandishing their spears, Phillip, with some of his officers, went ashore immediately to look for water. Before long he was confronted by some natives who were – very naturally – showing hostility. He immediately put down his weapons and, with his arms outstretched in friendship, he went alone towards them. They responded by putting down their spears.

If this gesture had been made only out of obedience to the British authority's instructions to act in a friendly way, it would never have had the effect it did have. Sincerity and fearlessness are a magical combination. If either of them had been lacking in Phillip, the first meeting might well have been a

FIRST FLEET ENTERING BOTANY BAY
From *The Picturesque Atlas of Australasia, 1886*

shedding of blood, mutual suspicion and lasting enmity. However, this gesture is a picture of the confidence that is possible between races that have completely different backgrounds and it can now be seen as a true expression of Phillip's whole attitude to life. He had an extraordinary trust in his fellow human beings and all the courage necessary to support that trust.

Natives of all countries would be sensitive to the difference between true friendship and the pretence of it. They would understand, for instance, that the giving of gifts means one thing when done by one man and quite another when done by another. If all who landed with him had been able to follow the example given by their leader, the story would have been completely different but that was impossible and no wonder! This quality, so well developed in Phillip, is still obviously undeveloped in the vast majority of people two hundred years later. It is the quality that makes the human being able to confront his fellow man – regardless of the incidental differences such as race, nationality, sex or status – as a human being. It seems to be of the greatest importance for the future that as many as possible do take it in deeply that the first act performed after Captain Cook had landed eighteen years before was an expression of fearless trust between two vastly different races. Because this happened and was genuine, this original gesture was the real beginning – the official one being held on the 26th.

BOTANY BAY

As Phillip's instructions were to land the convicts as soon as possible after arrival, his first concern was to explore the Bay so as to be able quickly to assess first the water situation, then the suitability of the land and the harbour. He was to find that the water supply was limited, there was not a lot of timber for building huts and the earth looked harsh and unfruitful.

In view of the fact that the two reports on Botany Bay seemed to be contradictory, it must also be mentioned that Cook and Banks saw the Bay in autumn and Phillip in the middle of summer. Many small possible areas were found but

CAPTAIN PHILLIP'S FIRST SIGHT OF PORT JACKSON
From *the Picturesque Atlas of Australasia, 1886*

nothing that could accommodate the large number of people Phillip had in his care with all their provisions.

THREE BOATS SAILING NORTH

After having decided to examine the coast further north where Cook had seen an opening and named it Port Jackson, he set out the day after Captain Hunter arrived on the *Sirius* with the rest of the fleet. He took three boats so that he would be able to explore this opening more quickly. In case he might not be able to find any suitable place for the settlement at Port Jackson, he left orders for Major Robert Ross – Lieutenant-Governor and Commander of the Marines – to supervise the clearing of the best of the land on Point Sutherland and for Lieutenant Gidley King of the *Sirius* to do further exploration of that part of the Bay that had not yet been explored.

The men in the three boats had to cope with a heavy, off-shore swell as they followed the coastline in the wake of Captain Cook.

Let us try to imagine the feelings of the Commander who had taken on the responsibility of the voyage to Botany Bay. He had been instructed to get the convicts off the ships as soon as possible on arrival and yet on arrival he had found that what had been thought suitable for the settlement was not suitable at all. There, anchored in the Bay, were the three storeships, the six transport ships and the two naval ships and here he was with a few men in a little boat sailing northwards. When he was about to pass between the rugged headlands of the opening that was to him only a speck on the map with the name Port Jackson attached to it, he might have wondered whether these few hours of sailing were leading to another delay and another disappointment for all.

PORT JACKSON

On going through the Heads and looking north and then south, he would have seen a good stretch of water with most of the surrounding hills covered with trees to the water's edge.

A VIEW OF BOTANY BAY
By kind permission of the Mitchell Library, Sydney

Then, turning south and making his first landing at what is now known as Camp Cove, he might have been somewhat disappointed. However, he sailed further south and it was then that he saw what he described as "the finest harbour in the world, in which a thousand sail of line may ride in the most perfect security." Then there was an exploration of many coves and bays. About one such place Phillip remarks:

> The boats, in passing near a point of land in the harbour, were seen by a number of men, and twenty of them waded into the water unarmed, received what was offered to them and examined the boats with a curiosity that gave me a much higher opinion of them than I had formed from the behaviour of those seen on Captain Cook's voyage, and their confidence and manly behaviour made me give the name of *Manly Cove* to this place. (pp. 23-24 *Select Documents in Australian History* Page 65. Phillip to Sydney 15th May 1788).

In this same despatch he went on to say,

> The different coves were examined with all possible expedition. I fixed on the one that had the best spring of water, and in which the ships can anchor so close to the shore that at a very small expense quays may be made at which the largest ships may unload. This cove I honoured with the name of *Sydney*.

EXCITEMENT AT BOTANY BAY

Phillip returned to Botany Bay on the 23rd. The reports from Ross and King were unfavourable, so he decided to move the fleet the next morning. However, this was not to be. Something happened that made him wait until the 25th. Captain Watkin Tench of the marines gives a graphic picture.

> The thoughts of removal banished sleep, so that I rose at the first dawn of the morning, but judge my surprise on hearing from a sergeant, who ran down almost breathless to the cabin where I was dressing, that a ship was seen

JEAN FRANCOIS DE GALAUP, COMTE DE LA PEROUSE
From *The Picturesque Atlas of Australasia, 1886*

LA PEROUSE' MONUMENT AT BOTANY BAY
From *The Picturesque Atlas of Australasia, 1886*

off the harbour's mouth. At first I only laughed, but knowing the man who spoke to me to be of great veracity, and hearing him repeat his information, I flew upon deck, on which I had barely set my foot, when the cry of "another sail" struck on my astonished ear. Confounded by a thousand ideas which arose in my mind in an instant, I sprang upon the barricade and plainly descried two ships of considerable size, standing in for the mouth of the Bay. By this time the alarm had become general, and every one appeared lost in conjecture. Now they were Dutchmen sent to dispossess us, and the moment after storeships from England with supplies for the settlement. The improbabilities which attended both these conclusions were sunk in the agitation of the moment.

It was by Governor Phillip that this mystery was at length unravelled, and the cause of the alarm pronounced to be two French ships, which, it was now recollected, were on a voyage of discovery in the southern hemisphere. Thus were our doubts cleared up, and our apprehension banished; it was, however, judged expedient to postpone our removal to Port Jackson, until complete confirmation of our conjectures could be procured.   . .

These two ships were under the command of Jean Francois de Galaup, known as La Perouse.

LA PEROUSE

La Perouse had joined the French Navy the year after both Cook and Phillip had joined the British Navy and all three had fought in the Seven Years' War. He was wounded and taken prisoner. It was as a prisoner-of-war that he made his one and only visit to England, where he was nursed back to health and came to admire his country's enemy.

It was in 1782, after France had joined the Americans in their battle for independence, that La Perouse was sent to Hudson Bay to destroy the British forts. This he did successfully but, in doing it, he left enough food and ammunition for the enemy so that, when they returned, they had shelter and the means of defending themselves against the natives of the land. He was not prepared to starve the English or leave them defenceless.

On the 1st August 1785 La Perouse sailed from Brest in the wake of Cook. Now that we know what happened at Botany Bay, it is interesting to learn that his start was delayed for three weeks because of adverse winds. It was a lavishly supplied expedition and there was an abundance of all their needs on the two ships. While at Kamtscharka in Russia, this great navigator replaced the board which marked the burial place of Captain Clerke who, after Cook's death, tried to carry out his wishes but died himself in the effort. It was at this port of call that he learnt of the British sending an expedition to Botany Bay.

He then sailed into the South Pacific and eventually to the Samoan Islands. He was anxious to take on water and food. Just before leaving and against his wishes but not against his command, many men went back onto the island. This time they were attacked by a large number of natives. Twelve were killed – one being the captain of the other ship – and all the others were wounded. Two of the ship's boats were lost.

It was with a heavy heart that La Perouse made his way to Botany Bay to make up two boats, the frames of which he had with him, and to get water. He first sighted the coast on the 22nd January 1788.

On the 24th, as the two ships were about to go through the entrance of the Bay, they were caught in winds and currents that took the ships south of the entrance and it was not until the morning of the 26th that they appeared again.

25th JANUARY

Phillip, being relieved by his certainty that it was the French ships on a voyage of exploration, obeyed his permanent sense of urgency and his orders from the Government and sailed to Port Jackson on the morning of the 25th. He left Captain Hunter to sail the rest of the fleet the next day with instructions "that they (the French) be shown the necessary marks for entering the harbour" (Tench).

When the French ships reappeared on the morning of the 26th, Hunter sent a lieutenant of the Navy to offer assistance and point out the necessary points for entering the Bay. Collins goes on to say, "As Captain Hunter was working out when La Perouse entered Botany Bay, the two commanders had barely time to exchange civilities."

The *Supply,* under the command of Arthur Phillip, sailed into Port Jackson during the afternoon of the 25th January. She was then anchored at Sydney Cove. Now, there was a slight pause – one night – between the sense of urgency about getting the fleet to its destination and the new sense of urgency about the fulfilling of his destiny.

Many hours would have been spent on the voyage thinking over his plans and by now he would have adjusted the plans to the shape of the small strip of land on which they would be carried out. Phillip would have to start at once on what would become a relentless round of decisions and commands and reflection on the results of them. He would have to be always changing his plans to fit in with the capabilities of all the people and making adjustments according to their feelings and actions. We can now see that the whole experiment would have been a hopeless failure unless he had been exceptionally adaptable, increasingly stable and ever ready to accept whatever conditions life would offer to such a group of people.

The night had come when he and his companions of the *Supply* would have their last sleep before being put to the test in an unknown land and in a practically unmanageable situation. Here they were, some thirteen thousand miles (21,000km) from home, on this small sailing ship, which was alone in the majestic harbour whose waters were part of a mighty ocean that was practically unknown. These men who had been buffeted about on so many stormy days and nights – some of them never having experienced life at sea before – must have enjoyed the sense of safety and the sound of the waters lapping gently against the shoreline of their new home. Many must have slept deeply till light came gradually flooding over everything at the dawn of the 26th January 1788.

THE FIRST FLEET ENTERING PORT JACKSON
By kind permission of the Mitchell Library, Sydney

Dawn of this day saw Arthur Phillip ready for action. He was about to take on what turned out to be one of the most terrible tasks imaginable. He had accepted complete authority of life and death over such an assembly of people. This must, in itself, have been a heavy load to bear. The only certainty would be that there would be continual uncertainty about what the day or the night would bring and continual strain and tension for the physical body that was already too strained and weakened to stand any testing task easily.

Every move he made would be watched, every decision would be open to criticism by people who would not have his purpose in view or his ability to see the overall picture. Every letter to the Home Government would take many months to bring a reply, if any, and there was no certainty that there would be any co-operation.

Here was a man of a sensitive, compassionate nature and a love of order and harmony faced with having to enforce discipline, knowing that the hardened criminals would almost certainly put him in a position of having to agree to hard sentences, including execution.

On this eventful day, he set going the work of clearing an area for the erection of a few tents and also an area for the raising of a flagstaff. In the afternoon, the ship's company saw the British colours hoisted. This was the official beginning of the development of a nation.

By the evening, the rest of the fleet had arrived and was anchored near the *Supply*. Some of those on deck were for the first time looking at the place where they would serve their time of transportation and others seeing the place where they would complete their term of office. The great moment had come when all the captains and crews of the ships had brought the first passengers safely to Port Jackson. All who had taken part in the first day's work returned to the *Supply* for the night.

DISEMBARKATION

Just imagine the scene as over one thousand people, who had been cooped up in such small spaces for so long, were, during the next eleven days, brought ashore.

They were not coming ashore to find houses and gardens ready to receive them as Phillip had hoped. No, there was nothing but tall trees hiding their new home from them and an unknown weather pattern. They were not exactly fired with enthusiasm for helping to fulfil the vision of their commander. They were, on the whole, a group of people not wanted in their own country, many of them mentally deranged, many of them diseased and many others were hardened criminals.

What a situation for a man who bore within him a vision that was never to leave him. He had been given very little of what he had thought necesary for him as a servant of that vision. Yet, till his death, he would always be a servant of it.

WORK STARTS

With the unloading of the ships, the peace of thousands of years was broken by the crash of the axe against trees and the clash of personality against personality.

The first task was to clear the trees from where Phillip had decided to set up tents, build huts and make gardens. In order that this job could be started at once, some marines and convicts were taken ashore on the first day and the rest, except, the women, on the following day.

The difficulty of clearing the ground was extreme. The wood of the trees was so hard that felling them with the best of tools would have taken a long time but it was soon found that the tools sent out were of the poorest quality. Not only were the tools of poor quality but the workers were lacking in energy and interest. By the end of the first year the convicts had cleared only enough to sow eight acres (about 3.25 hectares) of barley for the colony.

As the ground was cleared, tents were put up. Later, huts would be built out of unseasoned wood and also clay with cabbage-palms for the roofing. These dwellings were very temporary ones and, of course, subject to fire and giving little protection against weather.

While some were working on erecting these temporary dwellings, there was much other activity going on. Tools, equipment and stores that were required for immediate use were being unloaded. The stores had to be covered and guarded; forges, which were part of the scene in the villages of England and necessary for the colony, were being set up; places for cooking were being established and the marines were parading.

Only a few days passed before a typical Australian thunderstorm provided more incentive to work in those capable of it. Everybody could now feel that the need for better shelter was urgent. In this storm, some sheep were killed when a tree, under which they were sheltering in a shed, was struck by lightning. Another tree, near Phillip's canvas house, was also struck. This storm was described by Surgeon White as the worst he had ever experienced.

SURGEONS BUSY

Soon after landing, the dreaded scurvy, which had been kept at bay on the ships, broke out. The whole situation was made worse when many, including Phillip, got what was known as camp dysentery. The hospital tents had been erected and Phillip had more substantial shelters erected as soon as possible. There were no mattresses, sheets or blankets. It is easy to forget that, in those primitive hospitals, there were no painkilling drugs, antiseptic or taps to turn on for instant hot water or even cold. The situation was grim. White wrote:

> More pitiable objects were never seen. Not a comfort or convenience could be got for them, besides the very few we had with us. His Excellency, seeing the state these poor objects were in, ordered a piece of ground to be cleared for the purpose of raising vegetables for them.

The untended soil provided only a picking – not nearly enough for everyone – of wild parsley and spinach and a herb they called sweet-tea. Phillip had these picked for the sick.

LIEUTENANT-GOVERNOR

It was as early as this that the Governor realized that he would have little help and a lot of hindrance from Major Ross, the man appointed to be Lieutenant-Governor and Commander of the Marines. What a difference it would have made if Phillip could have chosen the man for this position but he had not been asked to choose any of the personnel for the settlement.

As Lieutenant-Governor, Ross must surely have realized that the British Government had not sent any qualified men to supervise the conduct and work of the convicts. It was obvious, then, that the military men under his charge would be the only men who could do this job with any sort of efficiency. Yet, when it was suggested that the military men did take on this work, Ross refused to allow them to do it. He said that they were taking their orders from England and that this had not been suggested as part of their work – that their job was to guard the colony. Guarding the colony would not have taken much effort or time at all if the convicts could have been kept away from the natives, instead of being free to steal from them. Although Ross was on the spot, he did not have enough insight to see that the Governor would need to be able to have the final decision on anything. He could not see that anything that might be decided in England might have to be able to be overruled by the man responsible for the success of the scheme.

As it turned out, there was very little soldiering to be done and, because of not having much to do, the marine soldiers became discontented and bored. Their main pastime was quarrelling. This meant that, right from the beginning, Phillip had to face this opposition that came from those who could have been most effectively helping him. It also meant that he had the permanent strain of having to be careful that he did not offend any of the military officers and it did not seem to take much to offend some of them.

THE CONVICTS OVERSEEING CONVICTS

The only thing left for Phillip to do was to give this job of overseeing the work and conduct of the convicts to those men amongst the convicts who had, on the voyage, shown that they would most likely be able to co-operate. It was very hard on Phillip that he had to ask the convicts to do this and very hard on the convicts that they had to be asked. He would, of course, have known that the work could not be done effectively, as the convicts could naturally be afraid of what would happen to them if they did try to restrain anyone going against the laws or if they did act as informers. All this meant that the work was incredibly slow, some convicts even hiding or breaking their tools so that they could not work. It also meant that there was more violence, more thieving and more wandering off into the bush than there would otherwise have been.

FIRST SURVEY OF THE HARBOUR

While Phillip was working to get order out of chaos during the first two weeks after landing, he was aware of how important it was for him to know as much as possible about the harbour. Having been unable to do much of it himself, he sent Captain Hunter, Lieutenant Bradley and James Keltie – all from the *Sirius* – to do a survey of it. This first survey started on 2nd February and finished three days later. From time to time after that, there was much surveying of the waters.

FIRST RELIGIOUS SERVICE

On Sunday the 3rd February, the Rev. Richard Johnson held the colony's first religious service in the shelter of a big tree. It was attended by the marines in full uniform and by those convicts who were ashore. Captain Watkin Tench, writing of the convicts says, "Their behaviour on the occasion was equally regular and attentive."

Some of the members of that first Australian congregation must have sent out thoughts of deep thankfulness for their

VIEW IN PORT JACKSON
By kind permission of the Mitchell Library, Sydney

46

safe arrival on that shoreline so far distant from their home-land. The thoughts and feelings connected with the thanksgiving about arrival in their new home would have had an influence for the good even if they were not sustained for long. For us, so used to the sense of security that comes from fast travel combined with easy, quick communication with the land, it is hard to imagine the sense of surprised relief that must have been felt by some of those standing under that tree, sharing, for once anyway, a common feeling.

FIRST WOMEN DISEMBARKED

It was on the eleventh day that the women convicts were brought ashore. This led to further stresses and strains. Against orders, many sailors came ashore and brought their ration of alcohol with them. Ugly scenes of drunkenness and uncontrollable self-indulgence were enacted without any delay.

The women convicts were separated into two groups. Those who showed signs of being more thoughtful and more capable of co-operating were put in one part of the Cove while those who were completely enslaved to their instincts and, by this time, more or less helpless, were put in another part. Phillip did not waste time and energy worrying about anything when nothing could be done about it.

FIRST GENERAL ASSEMBLY
PROCLAMATION DAY

It was not until 7th February that sufficient order was achieved to make it possible for Phillip to decide upon a place and a time for the assembling of the whole company – except for those on duty. This was Proclamation Day. When all the convicts, except the nine who were found to be missing, were assembled, they were asked to sit down. The Judge-Advocate, David Collins, then read His Majesty's Commission, the Act of Parliament for establishing courts in the colony and his instructions in great detail. The reading of these documents made it clear to everyone that Phillip was

CAPTAIN ARTHUR PHILLIP
First Governor of the Colony.   From *The Picturesque Atlas of Australasia, 1886*

the Captain-General and Governor-in-Chief over a very large area. It also set out all the guidelines on which the colony was to be founded.

It must be remembered that these details were instigated by Phillip himself as he, before leaving England, had had the commission re-written to include the details that he could foresee would be necessary.

As soon as Collins had finished reading all his documents, Phillip turned to the military and naval officers and thanked them for the way they had played their part in getting the ships safely to their destination, and then he turned and spoke to the convicts.

FIRST SPEECH TO THE CONVICTS

There are many versions of what Phillip said to that assembly but the differences are small compared with the similarities in them. The whole speech, however, would have been different in word and tone if Phillip had had the attitude to criminals that was common at that time. His attitude made him able to stand before these convicts as one human being to another, appealing to what goodness was in them, pointing out that they were facing a new opportunity if they would accept the necessary discipline to make something more of themselves. He let them know that he was only too anxious to bring them with him into a new set-up. He tried to make them feel that they were needed but he also made it quite clear that, if they would not accept the discipline that they themselves had made necessary, he would have to carry out his duty, no matter what effect it had on his feelings.

The trust in human nature that was part of Phillip's equipment for this job was very evident at this stage. He was different from legal and political authorities in England and from those working under his command. He did not think, "those convicts are criminals and, therefore, cannot change themselves except to become worse." He worked with the hope that some would become more willing to try to be more considerate for those who shared their fate and more truthful and so on. The disappointments did not make him lose this hope or lose his temper. If he had begun to despair of the people, despair would have won the day.

FIRST MARRIAGES

In his speech, Phillip also encouraged marriage so that some sort of stability might be brought into the chaotic situation. He did everything possible to stop the situation turning into an uncontrollable scramble for survival. It was said by one observer of the scene that it was a case of everyone for himself and the Governor for all. It was this everyone-for-himself motive that Phillip was anxious to change into something that would be in accordance with his feeling for what was to come in the future out of their common sufferings.

Although little notice was taken of the warning of severe punishment being given for offences, some notice was taken of his advice about marriage. During the next week, fourteen marriages were celebrated and during the second a further ten.

FIRST SIGNS OF LATER TROUBLE

A few days later, the commission was re-read to those who had been unable to hear the first reading of it. It was then that it became obvious that, amongst the military members of the group, there was resentment against Phillip because he had been given so much power. When feelings rush in before reason can get to work, then resentment, envy, jealousy, hatred or fear make it impossible for the people harbouring any of these feelings to think straight. Such feelings make the atmosphere unpleasant and strained – to say the least. So, it would be impossible for some to see that the scheme would not have been practical, if Phillip had not had the power he did have. On the other hand, it would have been possible for others to see that, in these circumstances, such power was necessary.

All naval men would know that many a ship that got safely home in the end would have gone to the bottom, if decisions had been left to more than one man. In real danger, it is not reasonable to say, "Wait a few hours till we get together and work out what should be done" or even to say, "Wait a minute till I see what so-and-so thinks." By that time, the situation would have changed and very possibly have brought about the death of all. Just as naval men are always in danger when at sea and not only when fighting in wars, so everybody at Sydney Cove was always in danger. It was a highly explosive situation. It would have been very easy for it to get completely out of hand. The undercurrents of uncontrolled human emotions and the storms brought about by violent and unpredictable actions against the community made it necessary for Phillip to be ready to make split-second decisions at any time of the day or night.

There is always hatred issuing from those who are anxious for the power but would not and could not stand the pain of power that is combined with compassion. So it is that the British Government performed a deed important for the future of Australia when it vested such power in a man worthy and able to bear it without using it for his own personal gains. It was just such power and the resentment against it that took such a heavy toll of the physical health. It was fortunate for everybody that all this strain did not sap his will or his ability to use it in service to his fellow men. The old catch-phrase, "Power corrupts and absolute power corrupts absolutely" takes no account of history and so makes a mistake that leads people away from accurate observation of life.

FIRST CRIMINAL COURT-SITTING

The Criminal Court was not, as in England, to be convened at certain times but when necessary as soon as possible after an offence was committed. This was related to the fact, that there was so much to get done just to save life and to achieve some sort of order. If those who had committed crimes had had to wait around under guard till a set date, there would have been worse trouble.

The Criminal Court, as set out in instructions, was to consist of the Judge-Advocate and six men of the sea or land services. Once again Phillip was to meet opposition. Major Ross informed him that he and his men were opposed to the taking part in any work of the court except in their own court. On the 16th May, in a despatch to Lord Sydney, the following statement is made:

The sitting as members of the Criminal Court is thought as hardship by the officers, and of which they say they were not informed before they left England. It is necessary to mention this circumstance to your Lordship, that officers coming out may know that a young colony requires something more from officers than garrison duty.

It might seem strange that the whole court procedure was set going in a few days on account of the small number of offences but it stands to reason that the sooner people could learn that Phillip meant what he said the better.

At the first sitting, on the 15th February, there were three offenders brought to trial. The first trial was for assault, the next for theft of food and the third for theft of an article. The first two were given their punishment but the third was let off by the Governor, who had power to mitigate or cancel a sentence. The Judge-Advocate himself recorded the following about this time:

> The mildness of these punishments seemed rather to have encouraged than deterred others from the commission of greater offences; for before the month was ended the criminal court was again assembled for the trial of four offenders, who had conceived and executed a plan for robbing the public store during the time of issuing provisions. This crime, in its tendency big enough with evil to our little community, was rendered still more atrocious by being perpetrated at the very time when the difference of provisions, which had till then existed, was taken off, and the convict saw the same proportion of provisions issued to himself that was served to the soldier and the officer, the article of spirits only excepted. Each male convict was that day put upon the following weekly rations, two-thirds of which was served to the female convicts, viz 7 lbs biscuit; 1 lb flour; 7 lbs beef, or 4 lbs pork; 3 pints of peas; and 6 ozs butter.
>
> It was fair to suppose that so liberal a ration would in itself have proved the security of the store, and have defended it from depredation; but we saw with concern, that there were among us some minds so habitually vicious that no consideration was of any weight with them, nor could they be induced to do right by any prospect of future benefit, or fear of certain and immediate punishment.

In Sydney, the stealing of food was punishable by execution. If it had not been so, Phillip would have been encouraging those who would steal food to bring about the slow death by starvation of those who would not steal.

The punishment was harsh indeed but everyone had been warned in public and there were criminals there whose criminal record was unknown, there were no prisons to keep them separate from the rest of the company and the rest of the company had to be protected.

With regards to the punishments it must be borne in mind that, as the historian George Mackaness said, "they were not Phillip's punishments". They were imposed according to the law of that time and the laws were made according to the thought of the day. He witnessed the punishment of the convicts as much as possible so that he could see that they were carried out as fairly and as humanely as possible. There were times when he said "no," to an execution sentence or reduced some punishments. He was one of those who, at that time, was working towards a different attitude towards criminals. However, he did not jump to far ahead of the thought-life of the past, nor did he shuffle along dragging the worst of the thought- life of the time with him.

He was doing all he could to help those who would co-operate in the building of the colony and there was in him nothing of the sense of superiority that was so common amongst the soldiers. He knew the task would be difficult; he knew that he had to supply food and protection but he also knew that he had to give the people something to work for, some encouragement; he knew he had to bring about some dignity where there was no external evidence of it. He had dignity within him and was not dependent on external evidence of it. So he was able to inspire the confidence that can be inspired by dignity, kindness and firmness.

PAINFUL EXPERIENCES

We could be helped to realize some of the difficulties of the job when we consider the description given by Surgeon Bowes of the very early days:

The anarchy and confusion which prevailed throughout the camp and the audacity of the convicts, both men and women, is arrived to such a pitch as is not to be equalled, I believe, by any set of villains in any other spot upon the globe. . . The men seize upon any sailors on shore who are walking near the women's camp, beat them most unmercifully, and desire them to go on board.

It was Clark, an officer of the marines, who said, "I hope this will be a warning to them from coming into the whores' camp. I would call it by the name of Sodom, for there is more sin committed in it than in any other part of the world."

Clark was the man who helps us to get another picture of the difficulties in the first colony. In his diary, in which he wrote daily to his wife, he gave the following graphic picture:

I was very ill with the toothache all last night. Got up early and went to the hospital – and had it out by Mr Consident. Oh, my God what pain it was. It was so fast in and the jaw bone very fast to one of the prongs, the tooth would not come out without breaking the jaw bone, which he did. I thought that half my head would have come off, there is a piece of the jaw bone remaining to the tooth. The pain was so great, my dear wife, that I fainted away and was very ill the remainder of the day, but I would not let Consident report to Major Ross that I was ill but would go on picket: my gum kept bleeding all the day.

There was much resentment amongst the soldiers and the sailors about the severity of their punishment compared with that of the convicts. It was unreasonable, as the soldiers' punishment was given by their officers and the sailors' by theirs and the convicts' was, as often as possible, under Phillip's direct control.

NATIVES

Just as Phillip's attitude to the convicts was different from that of the majority, so was his attitude to the natives different.

54

He respected them and showed no fear of them and he thought of them as a people who would listen to reason. He was always anxious to demonstrate justice to them. Of course, during the first year all this had to be done by action as there was no verbal communication between them. He wanted them to see that he knew that the guilt of any harmful deed lies at the door of the person who provokes the person to perform a harmful deed. In all cases of disturbance, he would try to find out who caused the trouble. He constantly found that the convicts were the aggressors. So, in order to demonstrate justice, he would, at first, have the convict punished, where possible in front of the natives. He realized, too, that the convicts would take advantage of the natives' lack of understanding of their language. They could give their point of view but the natives could not.

Although Phillip was instructed in his commission to maintain a friendly relation with the natives and to report to the Home Office any information he could find out about them, it would not have been possible for him to carry out those instructions in the way he did, if he had not had the ability to do this already strongly developed within himself. His actions seemed to be both natural and consistent.

At first, the natives were seen around the settlement watching with curiosity but, after a time, they were not seen very much at all. However, from time to time there was conflict between them and the sailors in the bush. The sailors were a cause of much disturbance as some of them were not above stealing the natives' equipment in order to sell it in England.

The tensions of feeling between the different sections of the community at Sydney Cove naturally made it impossible for Phillip to have the relationship he would have had with the natives if the people had all accepted the situation as it was, instead of complaining and filling the atmosphere with feelings of suspicion and antagonism.

H.M.S. SUPPLY   The *Supply* (170 tons) as she appeared after reconstruction in 1938
By kind permission of the Royal Australian Historical Society

NORFOLK ISLAND
(Latitude 29° south, Longitude 168° east
About 1000 miles (1600km) north-east of Sydney)

Instructions from England also required that colonization should start as soon as possible on the island named Norfolk Island by James Cook. He had reported that flax had been seen growing in abundance. In those days, flax was for the Navy an important plant, as it was used for the making of sails. On the 12th February, the day when Phillip's commission was re-read, Lieutenant Gidley King's commission was read. By this commission, he was instructed to begin cultivating flax as soon as the party was housed and the provisions under shelter. King was given restricted powers of justice and, as there were no means of setting up a court at Norfolk Island, any serious offence had to be tried at Sydney Cove. King had to send detailed reports of progress to Governor Phillip as often as possible.

So, Phillip was making the last minute plans, deciding how many people to send, seeing that the ship was in as good a condition as possible and loaded with necessities. On the 14th February, King sailed on the *Supply* under the command of Lieutenant Ball. The others, some of whom had volunteered to go, were a surgeon's mate, two officers, two private soldiers, two men who were thought to be familiar with flax-dressing and nine men and six women convicts. They had tents, farming implements, tools for dressing flax and provisions for six months.

The weather was boisterous. The voyage was rough and it took two weeks to sight the island. As they sailed round the coast and saw that the high cliffs rose straight up from the water's edge, they would surely have been agreeing with the description given by one of La Perouse's men. He described the island as "fit only for eagles and angels". There were reefs, too, that stopped them from getting the *Supply* into the shore. The ship was blown out to sea. The next day, King landed with a small party to find a suitable place for settlement. They spent the whole morning fighting their way through thick scrub and over high peaks to the other side of the island.

57

Then, trying to return to their base, they followed a stream and lost their way. Just as they had decided to spend the night on the island, King, standing on a peak, which he named Mount Pitt, saw their little boat waiting near the shore. They managed to get back to the boat before dark – all except the surgeon. He was too exhausted to walk the last short distance. He slept on the island on a bed of leaves.

It was not until the 5th March, a week later, that an opening in the reef was found. Finally, they found themselves on a beautiful sandy beach, with an area clear of trees. King decided that this would be the place for settlement. He called it Sydney Bay. So it was that, on the 6th March, the settlement was set up. Tents, provisions and all the rest were unloaded and the colours flew till night-fall, showing that King had taken possession of the island in the name of Britain.

What a different scene from the one they had left. The soil was good, rich, black loam and so it was easy to have hope of survival. Lieutenant Ball returned to the mainland in about a fortnight. On the way back, he called into the island they had seen on the way out and called it Lord Howe Island, after the Admiral of the Fleet, and explored it. They found it was uninhabited by human beings but there were a lot of turtles. They took some back to the settlement at Sydney Cove for fresh food, which was still very scarce in the colony.

WORK STILL GOING ON AT SYDNEY COVE

Clearing and building were still the main concern. Each convict was allotted a small piece of land to grow things for himself and Phillip, trying to give some interest and incentive to the work, set them all a certain time in which to complete their jobs for the day. If they finished early, they could then work on their own plots of ground. Many who did finish the set job in a shorter time spent their time straying in the bush. This often led to trouble between them and the natives.

There is much written about the day-to-day life at the Cove. There were the meetings with the natives; the offences committed by the convicts, the sailors and the marines; the trials and punishments; illnesses and depression; even the weather, which had marked effects on the whole situation. It was sometimes very hot, sometimes very cold, sometimes very wet. They had no way of avoiding the full effects of the weather on bodies that were feeling the results of the continual eating of stale salted meat and flour in which weevils had taken a long-term interest.

FIRST EXPLORATION

The settlement on Norfolk Island now established, Phillip was free to carry out his next instruction. This was to explore the country and to learn as much as he could about the natives. This instruction was very much in accord with his wishes. He had soon realized that the soil round the Cove and near the coast was far from satisfactory and that it was urgent that everything had to be done to find land suitable for cultivation. The need for food was a constant concern but he also wanted to get some feeling for the country and look for further opportunities to have contact with the natives. He spent a day inspecting the harbour, hoping to find a way inland but without success.

In spite of the fact that he was still suffering the after effects of the dysentery, it was only just over a month after their arrival when he set out again with supplies for seven days with a small party. They were in two boats. The intention was to go through the Heads of Port Jackson and sail north to Broken Bay and see whether there was any better soil there and then walk back. After rowing to Broken Bay, the first night was spent in the boats on the north side of the Bay. The next day was spent exploring this north side in the rain, only to find it was very marshy and not at all suitable for cultivation. However, they landed and pitched tents, they had great difficulty in drying their clothes. Although it was still raining, they crossed the Bay to the south side. Here it was found that the land was also no good for cultivation — high peaks, dense bush and rocky ground. However, of this branch of the Bay he made the remark that it was "the finest piece of water I ever saw". He named it Pitt Water after the Prime Minister of England.

After eight days of rain, during which they explored the area and had some interesting contact with some natives, they went back in the boats. All were feeling the effects of this expedition in the rain and it was during this first work of exploring that Phillip suffered 'a pain in the side' from which he was to suffer greatly for the rest of his time in Australia and for some time afterwards. It was thought that it was brought on by the combination of extreme fatigue and having to remain in wet clothes for so long. No suitable land was found for cultivation. The Lieutenant-Governor, back at the Cove, is reported as referring to these strenuous and risky expeditions, carried out in the season when mosquitoes and death-dealing snakes and spiders are abroad, as 'parties of pleasure'!

LA PEROUSE LEAVES

While all the settling was going on at Port Jackson, La Perouse had set up a stockade at Botany Bay and had built his two boats. It was reported at Port Jackson that the French had had to fire on the natives. This, of course, would have made it more difficult for the people at the Cove. The French also suffered the loss of their chaplain and naturalist, L'Abbé Receveur.

La Perouse and Phillip did not meet but Phillip sent a message to La Perouse telling him that, if he wanted to send any despatches to the French Ambassador in London, they could be sent on the first ship to return from Port Jackson. This was done. Before leaving, La Perouse gave instructions to one of his officers to warn Phillip of the exact location of the island on which the massacre of his men had occurred.

On the 10th March, five days earlier than he had planned, he slipped out of the Bay and he and his two beautiful ships and all who had so far survived the journey sailed into the unknown never to be seen again. It was not until 1826 that the wredkage of the two ships was sighted on a reef in the Santa Cruz group of islands in the Pacific.

PROGRESS

When Phillip returned from his expedition he found that the weather had been much the same as he had experienced. As a result there was an increase in the number of the sick. Hospital accommodation, other than tents, was started immediately. There was to be a ward for the troops and one for the convicts and a dispensary for the few medical supplies that were brought out. In all, the building was eighty-four feet by twenty-three (25.6m by 7m) and was situated on the west side of the Cove in what is, at present, George Street North, near Circular Quay.

About this time a great discovery was made in the camp. A man was found who not only understood the making of bricks but was willing to supervise a group of convicts. So a kiln was erected about one mile (1.6km)from the settlement where suitable clay had been found. There was one drawback, of course, and that was that the bricks had to be carried by the convicts to the settlement. Another difficulty associated with building was that there was no limestone to be found with which to make the mortar.

A wharf was being built for the landing of the stores. There must have been a lot of activity on the harbour, as much of the different kinds of material needed for building was collected from different parts of the harbour and fishing was going on every day, although at times very little was caught.

FIRST PLAN OF SYDNEY

Now that things were beginning to be more settled, Phillip laid out his first plan for the settlement. One can get a glimpse of the sort of town he wanted this place to become. Writing to Lord Sydney, he speaks of his plan:

> I have endeavoured to place all public buildings in situations that will be eligible hereafter, and to give a sufficient share of ground for the stores, hospitals, etc. to be enlarged, as may become necessary in the future. The principal streets are placed so as to admit a free circulation of air, and are

BRICKFIELD HILL AND VILLAGE ON THE HIGH ROAD TO PARRAMATTA
Edward Dayes (after Watling) Published 1812. By kind permission of The National Library of Australia, Canberra

two hundred feet (61m) wide. The ground marked for Govenment House is intended to include the main guard, civil, and criminal courts, and as the ground which runs to the southward is nearly level, and a very good situation for buildings, streets will be laid out in such a manner as to afford a free air, and when the houses are to be built, if it meets with your Lordship's approbation, the land will be granted with a clause that will ever prevent more than one house being built in the allotment, which will be sixty feet in front and a hundred and fifty feet in depth (18.3m by 45.7m). This will preserve uniformity in the buildings, prevent narrow streets, and the many inconveniences which the increase of inhabitants would otherwise occasion hereafter.

ANIMALS

Before leaving England, Phillip had realized the need to build up the livestock in the colony. Human beings cannot manage without the help of animals, so some animals would have to suffer the journey too. With this in view, he and the officers had bought up as much livestock as possible at the Cape. After they were landed, they still had very hard times. At first, the public stock was put to graze on the eastern side of the Cove and when they had grazed that grass they were moved to what is now called Farm Cove. In the storm, some sheep were killed; many animals were lost as a result of eating rank grass; some were killed by dogs; some were stolen by the natives and in July the remaining public cattle strayed away from the convict who was looking after them. At that time, it must have seemed like near disaster but the cattle finally found good grazing and were found eight years later, increased in number.

An area near where the bricks were being made was cleared in order that those officers who had livestock could grow some grain for feed. Collins gives a picture of difficulties with the animals when he tells us:

Great inconvenience was found from the necessity that subsisted of suffering the stock of individuals to run loose amongst the tents and huts; much damage in particular was sustained by hogs, who frequently forced their way into them while owners were at labour, and destroyed and damaged whatever they met with.

STILL IT GOES ON AND ON

At any time, trouble could occur between the convicts and natives. Convicts would come in wounded from the bush, where they should not have been, telling tales about the natives but Phillip always suspected that it might have been the convicts who had provoked the natives to anger. The convicts used to steal the fishing gear and spears or whatever they could find and sell them to the sailors. So, Phillip had to make another law to prevent people buying from the convicts or selling to them and to give harsh punishment to the offenders. It is interesting that, when he returned from his expedition to Broken Bay, he saw some natives who seemed to him to be more shy than usual. When he had coaxed one to come near him, the native used signs to let Phillip know that he had been hit on the shoulder. It was another case of aggression by the convicts.

EXPLORATIONS

The sense of urgency about the need for better soil grew greater and greater. So, although he would have known that his absence from the Cove could make for more trouble there, Phillip set out with another party as early as the 15th April to explore inland.

The journey was so strenuous that he had to send Ball and a marine back with two sailors, who became too exhausted to go on. Phillip had noticed "a passage with deep water into a branch of the harbour that runs to the north west" (*Curl Curl Creek* – J.F. Campbell). He wanted to follow it to its source. In spite of his state of health, he waded waist-deep through water twice in an effort to find the source but had to turn back. After a change of course, the men came to what is now called Manly Lagoon or Harbord Lagoon. Turning west, they faced dense bush and tall trees. This was what is now known as Frenchs Forest. They camped the night by a swamp which was actually the source of the creek for which they had been searching. Still there was no sign of good soil. They came to Middle Harbour where they spent the night. White describes the place as "this most desert wild and solitary seclusion". As they were finding their equipment heavy, they decided to leave it at this camp site and push on. They then walked from Middle Harbour through Frenchs Forest, Turramurra, Thornleigh and on to the range on which the Great Northern Road now runs. Phillip tells of what he saw:

> We had a fine view of the mountains inland, the northernmost of which I named Caermarthen Hills and the southernmost Lansdowne Hills. A mountain between I called Richmond Hill and from the rising of these mountains I did not doubt but that a large river would be found. (*Hist. Rec. of Australia.* series 1. vol 1, pp.28.)

Weary of the endless bush, they turned back but still had hard walking to do, wading in parts where the tide had risen and, in other parts, having to climb heights which at first seemed impenetrable.

Back at the Cove, Hunter, thinking that they might need help to get back to the Cove, sent two boats to meet them at the place from which they had started. They speak about the "great satisfaction and comfort" they got from an unexpected meal.

As Phillip was sure that there must be a large river not far away, he allowed himself only six days before setting out again with the same party with the addition of a marine officer. He planned that they would be out for seven days and that each would carry his own needs and that the soldiers would carry the camping equipment. This time, they headed west but, because of the thickness of the scrub, they made little progress the first day. That night there was a big thunderstorm and they were wet, cold and overtired. Phillip had another attack of severe pain in his side. As he would not go back, they pushed on, sowing seed wherever they found a suitable spot.

BOTANY BAY HARBOUR, IN NEW SOUTH WALES: WITH A VIEW OF THE HEADS.
Drawn by J. Eyre. Engraved by W. Preston. Published 1812. By kind permission of The National Library of Australia, Canberra

As they went, it was found that the soil was improving, and the trees were further apart and there was less scrub. On the fifth day, they came to a hill which he called Belle Vue, (Prospect Hill) as from there he saw country " as fine as any I ever saw". Still the range of mountains he had seen on his previous expedition was estimated to be a further thirty miles (48km) away. As provisions were running low, he decided to return the way they came and on the return journey he was to say, "I believe, no country can be more difficult to penetrate into than this is." It was after this expedition that he decided to make another settlement at the head of the harbour where he had seen that the soil was better and the trees further apart. This did not take place till November. He had hoped to explore this area again soon but his state of health and the pressure of work at the Cove prevented it.

THE FIRST MONTH OF MAY

During the first ten days of May, three transport ships left, taking the first despatches from Australia.

Thefts, efforts to escape and assaults and other forms of crime were taking place and offenders being tried and punished.

The endless punishments Phillip had to witness would have caused him great grief but he knew that discipline was a necessity for the survival of the colony.

On the 30th May, an episode occurred which caused him to go to Botany Bay. Two convicts, while up the harbour cutting rushes for roofing, were savagely murdered and their tools had been stolen. Phillip decided that, if he were able to find the tools, he would be able to find the culprits. He was, as usual, aware that the convicts might well have been the ones who started the trouble. In going to Botany Bay, his intentions were to try to find the natives, show them his displeasure and also to find out why it took place.

While at Botany Bay, Phillip found the grave of the L'Abbé Receveur. Noticing that the wooden board nailed to a tree had been taken down and broken, he ordered a copper plate to be inscribed to replace it. In this connection, it should be remembered La Perouse replaced the inscription on the grave of Captain Clerke.

On returning from Botany Bay, Phillip and his companions came suddenly upon a great number of natives gathered together at the mouth of a cave. They were only about ten yards away when they noticed them and Phillip had little time to stop his men before a number of armed natives appeared. The one who seemed to be the leader came towards them making signs for them to get away but, when he saw Phillip advancing alone and unarmed, he dropped his spear and the two men met in a friendly way. It was no time before the white men found they were surrounded by about two hundred natives. However, there was no incident. They put down their spears and they were all peaceable. Had Phillip not spontaneously reacted as he did, there could have been disastrous results. Here a very good stream was found. When the natives found that the party was travelling north, an old native came forward and made signs to go ahead. As they approached the next cove, this native signalled those in the next cove, indicating that those coming were friendly. Phillip did not go into this cove but did see more natives. There were more in this area than he had expected. He also saw signs of fire on a hill to the west, on the hill he had called Lansdowne Hills.

CUMBERLAND COUNTY

On the 4th June, the celebrations for the King's birthday were finished with a dinner given by the Governor for the officers of the sea and the land and other officials. Phillip named a certain area Cumberland County. It was the largest County in the world, stretching from Broken Bay to Botany Bay and west to the hills he had seen on his expeditions. It was, in writing about this day, that White said:

> The day was spent in cheerfulness and good-humour; but it was a little damped by our perceiving that the governor was in great pain, from a return of his complaint. Though his countenance too plainly indicated his torture which he

suffered he took every method in his power to conceal it, lest it should break in upon the festivity and harmony of the day.

MORE PROBLEMS

Phillip was always facing new problems. There were some convicts who had no idea how to make their rations spin out over the week, rations being given out weekly. Some ate almost all theirs all at once and then stole because they were hungry. Of one convict it is told by Collins that he made all his flour into eighteen cakes weighing eight pounds (3.6kgm) and ate the lot at one time. The result was that he became "speechless and senseless and died the following day at the hospital." Another, in an effort to get money for his return passage to England, sold his rations and died of starvation. As winter approached, there was an increasing urgency to get shelters finished. However, the lack of suitable material and the difficulty in acquiring it slowed things down again and, even after six months, only four officers were in huts.

All carpenters were hired from the ships and as many as possible found amongst the convicts were working in that capacity. Instead of so much parading, the marines were spending more time building their own huts, cultivating the plot of land they had been allotted but they were discontented because Phillip would not take convicts from the public works, which were far behind in construction, to help them clear and cultivate their land. As it was, the carrying out of the public works was already hampered enough by the quality of the wood, the difficulty of getting it and the shortage of men skilled in the art of carpentry.

July was a busy month preparing for the sailing of the rest of the transport ships and a storeship. They would take back to England more despatches as well as specimens of animals, birds and plants etc. What seeds were available were collected. Tench admits that most of these early despatches from officers, marines and convicts gave a grim account of what had taken place, while the man who had most to complain about wrote despatches that had an air of hope about them.

However, his despatches did more than give the Home Office the information they required. They were also meant to be a means of helping those not in the situation to get some idea of what was needed. He made continual pleas for more overseers, artificers, farmers, carpenters, good tools and – most urgent of all – stores and free settlers. He pointed out the danger of putting people on one ship and stores on another, as it could happen that the people arrived without the stores. He let them know stores would have to be sent at regular intervals and that it would be some time before this country would be able to provide for all.

Another disappointment that caused great concern was the failure of the crops. Most of the seeds that had been collected on the way out and nearly all of what they had brought from England had not grown to maturity. Some came up, looked promising and then withered. Other seed did not even germinate, as much of the seed had rotted or germinated before sowing. What crops did mature had to be kept for seed for the next year and did not relieve the food shortage. The public stock was nearly depleted.

It was at this time that Phillip, with a small party of men, did an overland expedition to Broken Bay, reaching what is now known as Barrenjoey Headland.

During the first two weeks of August, the weather was very wet and many huts were damaged to such an extent that it took longer to fix the damage than to build another. No work on the public buildings was done, the brick kiln fell in and the roads were blocked. The barracks, the observatory, the Governors and the Lieutenant-Governor's houses were still in progress and the hospital was having its roof shingled. Thefts increased, quarrels went on and on. There was a big quarrel between two surgeons, which led to a duel and another beween Major Ross and one of his officers when one of the marine officers died.

THE *SIRIUS* SAILS OUT

With the failure of the crops and very little addition to the existing stores, Phillip became very concerned about the future supply of food. He did not have enough seed for future crops and he did need more stores, so he finally made the decision to send Captain Hunter in the *Sirius,* to the Cape of Good Hope, in spite of the fact that he only had the two naval ships at his disposal and the *Supply* was committed to making frequent voyages to Norfolk Island. He expected Hunter to be away about six months but, as it turned out, he was away seven months and six days. He was to get a year's stores for the *Sirius*, whatever flour he could stow away and enough grain for sowing for the next year. Early in October, after making all preparations, Hunter sailed out of Port Jackson. His journal gives a vivid description of one of the many dangers that he and the crew survived on that round-the-world voyage. He gives an account of a situation they found themselves in on the southern coast of Tasmania.

> I now found that we were embayed, and the gale not in the least likely to abate, and the sea running mountains high with very thick weather, a long dark night just coming on, and an unknown coast I only may call it (for although it has been seen by several navigators, it is not yet known) close under our lee. . . Our situation was such that not a man could have escaped to have told where the rest suffered. . . It would be the highest presumption and ingratitude to Divine Providence were we to attribute our preservation wholly to our best endeavours: his interference in our favour was so very conspicuously manifested in various instances, in the course of that night, as I believe not to leave a shadow of doubt, even in the minds of the most profligate on board, of his immediate assistance.

SECOND SETTLEMENT

On the 2nd November, Phillip went with the Surveyor-General, Augustus Alt, and several others to where he had decided to establish a second settlement. The area was chosen and marked out as to where the different buildings would be put up. Two days after this, ten convicts were sent up and the ground for the first shelters was cleared. Phillip named the settlement Rose Hill after Sir George Rose, Secretary to the

Treasury. Over the next month more convicts were sent. The officers and marines were then joined by a captain who had been made a Justice of the Peace and given the authority to give punishment for idleness and petty offences.

From time to time, Phillip received news from Norfolk Island. He had sent a storeship there in September and it returned in November, bringing Phillip news from King that all were well, that they had plenty of fish and vegetables and that the last crop sown looked promising.

CONCERN ABOUT NATIVES

The next big question for Phillip was what to do to get some relationship with the natives. There still was no verbal communication between the white and the black people and, in spite of all attempts, there had been no voluntary move from the natives to try to have any verbal contact.

Phillip records in a despatch to Lord Sydney on the 12th February 1790: (Hist. Rec. of Aust. 145)

> Not succeeding in our endeavours to persuade some of the natives to come and live with us, I ordered one to be taken by force, which was what I would gladly have avoided, as I know it must alarm them, but not a native had come near the settlement for many months, and it was absolutely necessary that we should attain their language, or teach them ours, that the means of redress might be pointed out to them if they are injured, and to reconcile them by showing the many advantages they would enjoy by mixing with us.

Tench describes the dilemma Phillip was in and also the steps he took:

> Tired of this state of petty warfare and endless uncertainty, the governor at length determined to adopt a decisive measure by capturing some of them, and retaining them by force; which he supposed would either inflame the rest to signal vengeance, in which case we should know the worst, and provide accordingly: or else it would induce an inter-

72

course, by the report which our prisoners would make of the mildness and indulgence with which we must use them.

On the 31st December 1788, Ball and Johnston went in two boats to Manly Cove and after a struggle captured one native and took him back to Sydney Cove. At first, he let out shrill shrieks but, when given some broiled fish, he settled down.

Back at the Cove, he was washed, clothed, fed and put in charge of a convict at night.

1789

On New Year's Day, the Governor gave a dinner and all the naval, marine and civil officers were invited and so was Manly. This was the name given to the captured native until somebody found out what his name was. He, like all his companions of the wide open spaces, was used to going for long periods without any food and, when it was available, he was used to eating large quantities. So it was that, after having eaten about eight pounds (3.6kg) of fish for breakfast, he, at this next meal, ate a further large serving of fish and meat. It was at this meal too, that he was first offered the white man's alcohol but he showed disgust at the smell and taste of it and would not drink anything but water. After this hearty meal and while music was being played, Manly stretched himself out on a chest under the window, put his hat under his head and went off to sleep. For Phillip, nothing could have been a better sign that Manly had already overcome the suspicions and fear that he had naturally expressed when he was being captured.

It was not for about a month that it was discovered that his name was Arabanoo. Progress was slow in achieving the aims of his capture. Some were able to learn a little of his language but, at this stage, nothing was achieved as regards relationship between the two races.

The first month of 1789 was very hot, the temperature reaching 105° (40.6C). Phillip was forever pleading for free settlers, at one time saying that, if only he could have fifty families interested in work, things would improve quickly. Free settlers and more provisions and implements were still his most desperate needs but he managed to continue without them, putting up with all the increasing hardships that resulted from his not having them. There was nothing going into the storehouses from the settlement and the awful absence of ships from England meant that the provisions were being reduced daily.

THREATENING INCIDENT

One day, Major Ross went to Phillip to inform him that one of his captains had died. The Governor replied that his adjutant was next in line for the position and that he would do without an adjutant. Then Ross, without mentioning his intentions, went straight to Collins and offered him the position, saying that Lord Howe had told him to do so. If Collins had wanted to escape his painful duties, to have less serious responsibilities in a better situation and fit in with the Lieutenant-Governor's opposition to the Governor, the colony would have been in a state of crisis. There was nobody else who could have filled the position held by Collins. As Ross would have known this, the incident shows that his hatred was not only a matter of feeling but of determination to try by every means to give the death-blow to Phillip's governorship. The incident also shows up the fact that temptations could be offered to induce those carrying out special tasks to join Ross against Phillip and that Phillip could, at any moment, be utterly dependent on some decision made by one of his officers.

EMPTY HARBOUR

When, in mid-February, the *Supply* sailed for Norfolk Island, taking 21 men, 6 women convicts and 3 children, who were wards of the State, the harbour was empty of ships for the first time since their arrival. The feeling of separation from the world must have been acute. There would be the thought that, if anything happened to the *Supply,* they would even be separated from the Norfolk Island part of the company. Thinking also of their situation if any foreign ships should arrive, Phillip had one of the bays surveyed so that any ship entering the harbour could anchor there. He named it Neutral Bay.

SEVERE SHOCK

In March, an incident occurred that shocked the whole colony. It was detected that seven marine soldiers had been systematically robbing the storehouse for several months. The law had to be enforced. All had been warned that stealing food was the most serious crime and punishable by execution. So it was that six of the seven soldiers were executed. The seventh was let off because there was no evidence found to show he was implicated.

TRAGEDY

The building of the barracks was more or less completed and a much bigger brick kiln had been built. Those whose jobs took them to different parts of the harbour daily reported seeing bodies of natives lying in caves, on the rocks and on the beaches. For a time the cause was not known but, when some were brought to the Cove, it was discovered to be smallpox. Of the newcomers, only one sailor died of the disease but many natives succumbed, including Arabanoo. Amongst those who recovered, were two children who were taken in, one by the Rev. Johnson and the other by John White. For a time they lived with the white people.

THE *SIRIUS* RETURNS

The sight of the *Sirius* entering the harbour at the beginning of May brought a sense of tremendous relief but it only lasted for a short time. There were supplies on board but only enough flour to last the colony four months in addition to a year's supply for the *Sirius* and seed for sowing the following year. These provisions had been secured at great risk to the lives of Captain Hunter and the crew. They had encountered some bad storms on their trip to and from the Cape. As a result of sailing right round the world for these supplies, the ship was so badly damaged that it took some months to make her seaworthy again. During these months, Hunter did much surveying work at Botany Bay and Broken Bay.

FIRST STAGE PLAY

The King's birthday was again celebrated on the 4th June and it was on this day that the first play was enacted in Australia. The convicts put on a comedy in a barn and gave the proceeds to the family of a soldier who had recently drowned.

DISCOVERY OF THE HAWKESBURY

On the 6th June, Phillip again set out on an expedition with the same purpose, that is of finding suitable land for cultivation. This time he took Hunter and a small party. A few went by boat to take provisions and the rest of the party walked. They left Port Jackson at 6 a.m. and arrived at a beach on the south side of Broken Bay at 3 p.m.. Hunter gives the following description of this part of the journey:

> It was a pretty warm, fatiguing journey, loaded as we were with provisions for several days, water and ammunition: we proceeded along the sea coast to the northwards: in the course of our march, we had many long sandy beaches to cross, which was a very fatiguing part of the journey: when we ascended the hills, we had frequently thick woods to pass through, but as we often fell in with paths, which the natives in travelling along the coast had trod very well down, these paths rendered our march, not only on account of pointing to us the most easy way and accessible parts of the hills and woods, but, in point of direction, the shortest which could be found, if we had even been better acquainted with this tract.

As the boats had already arrived, the first day was spent exploring the part that Phillip had named Pitt Water. The next

76

days were spent examining the many branches of the Bay. Before camping the night on a marshy point Phillip and Hunter had rowed up a particular branch for most of the day. As they were then about twenty miles (32km) from the Bay and as the water was some three to seven fathoms (5.5 − 12.8m) deep and two to six hundred feet (182m) wide, they had the joy of realizing that they had discovered a major river.

The next day, Phillip and Hunter returned to the Bay. The boats were loaded and sent back at midnight. Then, those remaining made a wigwam as shelter and set out the next morning to walk back to Port Jackson. They arrived there about two in the afternoon and on the 16th June joined up with the boats that were already there.

In spite of all his commitments and in spite of the prospect of excessive fatigue, Phillip was determined to return as soon as possible to follow that river to its source. So it was that, on the 29th June, he set out again with the same party and a few extra men. Their first stopping place was the head of Pitt Water but, because there was no boat in sight, they had to walk from there round all the bays, through woods and swamps to the branch they were going to explore. This trek was a big test of interest in discovery. Here they joined the boats and, by night of the next day, they had reached the point where they had camped the previous time. For the next few days they followed the main river as well as the three branches, the Macdonald, the Colo and Grose rivers, finally reaching Richmond Hill. This area looked more promising. Phillip named the large river they had been following the Hawkesbury.

They got safely back to the north side of Port Jackson − the Cove being on the south side − on the 13th but they found no boat to meet them. They spent the night by a large fire and the next day walked to Middle Harbour but could not cross the water. They fired shots to try to attract the attention of anyone who might be around. They found a canoe and thought that, if they could cross the fairly narrow strip of water, it was not far to walk over the hills to where the *Sirius* was being repaired. However, the canoe sank and their effort to build a light catamaran also failed. Hunter was thinking of another scheme when two of the men offered to swim across

VIEW OF PORT JACKSON TAKEN FROM SIRIUS ISLAND
Sirius lying off entrance of Sydney Cove Captain John Hunter, 1789

the span of water and then walk to the *Sirius*. This was in the winter month of July and they were suffering from malnutrition. This was finally done and eventually a boat was sent to take the weary travellers home. On this trek, they tracked down the sail-maker of the *Sirius*, who had been lost for four days. They fed him frequently on small bits of food and he soon recovered.

AT ROSE HILL

At this time, Tench, who was stationed at Rose Hill, went on an exploration trip with a small party from Rose Hill and, within a couple of days, he also discovered a large river west of Prospect Hill. Even then, it was suspected that this river and the one Phillip had discovered were one and the same but it had to be proved. Phillip named Tench's discovery the Nepean.

Henry Dodd was appointed superintendent of the Government Farm there. This appointment tells us a lot about both Phillip and Dodd, who came out as Phillip's servant. Phillip would know from experience that those who can be good servants are the best at giving orders and he had in his home somebody who was not only good at taking orders but also good at using his initiative and who had some experience of farming. So, it is not surprising that he appointed this man to this important position, though he would have been at a loss himself. Henry Dodd proved able to gain the respect of the convicts, to improve the work output and to be able to allot the punishment — that is to do the carrying out of the effort at justice that was the law in those days. He must have been an enormous help to Phillip in that capacity. In him the Governor had a friend and ally who proved able to get things moving at Rose Hill. Usually in a situation that works towards the future, there are a few who work helpfully behind the scenes and there must have been some men and women supporting the effort made by this man.

FIRST POLICE FORCE

The next month saw the end of the extra supply brought from the Cape. The days and nights, the weeks and months were slowly passing and still no word from England. It was becoming obvious that all were thinking that they had been forgotten. Hunger increased and so did thieving even from the gardens, which were, as early as this, being robbed at night.

With the increasing hardship and the decreasing hope, many convicts became worse in their conduct and attitude but some became better and were able to co-operate more. One wonderful bit of co-operation came from a convict by the name of Harris. This man went to Collins and suggested that perhaps it would help if some of the convicts could guard the settlement at night. This was passed on to Phillip who took up the suggestion at once and started the first Police Force. The whole area was divided into four sections and each section had three guards, each armed with staves. They were given the right to arrest anyone wandering around after the allotted time, to visit places that could attract trouble and to interfere with gambling and wrongful selling of clothes and provisions. Phillip promised them that their time of sentence would be reduced if they worked honestly and well and that anyone who did not would be severely punished. The scheme as a whole worked well. Some would undoubtedly have worked well without the promises but Phillip would have known that they would be a necessary aid to others.

As usual, he had to put up with opposition from Major Ross who complained that a convict had arrested a marine and he did not think this sort of thing was good enough for the military. So, in spite of the fact that marines had robbed the stores, he withdrew the clause that gave the convicts the right to arrest anyone. The chosen convicts worked so well and they had such an effect that Collins was to make the following remark: "It might possibly be asserted with truth, that many streets in the metropolis of London were not so well guarded and watched as the small but rising town of Sydney."

The whole affair between Phillip, the convicts and Ross shows up the fact already indicated that it is wrong to let the word 'convict' suggest that the person is necessarily worse in any way than somebody who is not a convict. There are vast differences between different convicts as there are between people who have never been in prison. Here were some of the people who were supposed to be a hindrance to society initiating and carrying out the dangerous work that the military personnel – at that time holding very high status – would not do.

VARIED EXPERIENCES

A boat on which to carry things between Rose Hill and Sydney became a necessity. A few convicts tried their hand at it and produced something that did the job but it was so heavy with wood that, although it was named *The Rose Hill Packet*, they nicknamed it *The Lump*.

As if there were not enough troubles, Phillip had to face the fact that rats had got into the storehouse and destroyed a large amount of flour, more or less overnight. He had all the stores moved into one of the rooms erected for the barracks and then had dogs put into the storehouse to catch the rats. Those rats that escaped got into the gardens and continued their work there.

In November, the food rations for men were reduced to the same as the women's and soon it was to be issued twice weekly instead of once as so many convicts consumed their rations too quickly.

Phillip, now anxious to reduce the number of mouths to be fed at the Cove, sent a further 14 convicts to Norfolk Island with orders for Lieutenant Ball to collect turtles from Lord Howe Island on the way back. Anything that could be eaten was welcome by those hungry people.

December of the second year brought no sign of relief from the threatened starvation. What harvest there was had to be kept for seed for the next sowing. This would not have made the Governor's interest in the future popular. From Norfolk Island there was good news, for King wrote to say that he hoped to have not only enough seed for next sowing but also enough tor food for about four months but, for the company at the Cove, the *Supply* brought only three turtles.

Still anxious to explore inland, Phillip sent a small party to try to penetrate the Caermarthen mountains but they were forced back by practically impenetrable bush. They were only able to travel fourteen miles (22km) in four days.

That was the last of the explorations for some months, as the colony as a whole was beginning to suffer the real effects of this shortage of food. No longer was it practical to send the usual men to Botany Bay, as had been done since arrival, to look out for any ships. Phillip was soon to carry out Hunter's suggestion to put a flagstaff on South Head to alert any shipping as to where the settlement was. The men of the *Sirius* were allotted the task of manning it. Some realized that this was of no practical use but, as it was a symbol of expectation of something that could come, it had a helpful effect.

BENNELONG AND COLBEE

Still anxious to establish a language relationship with the natives, Phillip sent Bradley to see if he could bring in another two. Although Bradley was not happy to do this, he did it well and brought two fine looking young men to the Cove. They were Baneelon (known now as Bennelong) and Colbee. It was soon discovered that they had enormous appetites and it was difficult not to let them know of the shortage of food amongst the settlers. Colbee escaped shortly after being brought in and Bennelong lived in the settlement for about six months.

1790

The first six months of 1790 surely must have been the most dramatic in the history of this land. The Governor doggedly set about doing all he could to prevent complete despair and failure. He set up an experiment to see how long it would take for a person to become self-sufficient. James Ruse, a convict who had served his term, was granted 30 acres (12 hectares) of land and so became the first free settler.

In February, Phillip had Lord Howe Island explored but found it not suitable for settlement. When the *Supply* returned from Norfolk Island, the news of the settlement there was such that Phillip decided to send more people there so that, if stores ran out in Sydney, there would be a chance of more people surviving. So it was that Phillip made a reshuffle, deciding to send Hunter in the *Sirius* in search of more provisions, after taking others to Norfolk Island; send Lieutenant Gidley King to England, taken by Hunter to his first port of call, to speak on behalf of the colony; send Major Ross as Governor of Norfolk Island. We can now see that this move would serve a double purpose of giving Ross some satisfaction for his desire for more authority, at the same time improving the atmosphere at the Cove. A further 116 men and 67 women convicts, 27 children and two companies of marines with their provisions were sent with them to the Island.

The *Sirius* and *Supply* left on the 6th March. The rains came, adding to the misery. Many huts were damaged, including the new guard house. Phillip's continual concern about the future led him at this time to forbid the killing of any livestock, excepting that which had belonged to those sent to the Island. A false rumour was spread, saying that all stock was going to be taken for public use. As a result of this, those who owned stock decided to kill what they had as well as what belonged to those who had gone, making out that what they killed belonged to these people. For Phillip this was just another serious setback.

This month, the ration was reduced again and was to be issued every day. This meant, too, that the hours of work had to be shortened again. Not only did the convicts continue to steal under these conditions but the animals that remained were very hungry and naturally did their share of robbing the gardens. Still it rained and more huts were damaged. The wooden storehouses began rotting so a new brick one was started. One of the marine officers lost his reason. One can wonder what else could possibly happen to make things worse but happen it did.

SIRIUS WRECKED

On the 5th April, a sail was seen. It turned out to be the *Supply* returning from Norfolk Island with the news that the *Sirius* had been wrecked on the coast of the Island. It had arrived there a week after leaving the settlement but it had taken days to get the personnel landed safely. Hunter and the crew had had a hard battle to get them ashore at all.

Immediately afterwards, the wind changed direction and the ships were blown out to sea with the provisions and animals still on board and it was days before they were able to get to the bay where the settlement was. The weather abated for a short time and some provisions were got ashore but there was still much of it on board when the wind changed again and the ship was dashed onto the reef. Though much private property went to the bottom, their struggle to rescue the stores and animals was partly successful. In the fury of the effort to get the human beings off the ship before it was too late, Hunter shoved Major Ross into a boat loaded with pigs, geese, fowls, turkeys, coal and other articles for use on the Island. Though he was criticized for not giving Ross the treatment due to him on acount of the importance of his position, he was making every effort to save as many people and provisions as possible when the ship was being wrecked.

The wreck of the *Sirius* meant that there were now five hundred and six people on the Island on half rations. Martial law was brought into force and much hardship was to be experienced before relief arrived in August.

BACK AT PORT JACKSON

At Port Jackson, because he knew that everyone could reasonably think they were facing the probability of death by hunger, Phillip called a council of all officers to discuss the situation and it was decided to send the *Supply* to Batavia – their last hope. She was to bring what she could of eight months' supply and hire a Dutch ship to bring the rest.

Lieutenant King went on the *Supply* to Batavia to pick up a ship to England taking with him the latest despatches.

The rations had been lowered to 2½ lbs flour, 2 lbs rice and 2 lbs meat a week. It must be remembered that Phillip, though he had to bear the greatest strains of all, had handed over for public use all his own stores and had put himself on the same rations as all the others. There was also a shortage of clothes and of the marines Tench writes:

> Many a guard have I seen mount, in which the number of soldiers without shoes exceeded that which had yet preserved remnants of leather.

Those who want to get some feeling for the hardships the whole company endured will be helped mostly by those who went through it. The following was written by a convict:

> We have so many disappointments about arrivals etc. that the sullen reserve of superiority has only increased our apprehension, and some of the ignorant have no other idea than that they are to be left by the troops and the shipping to perish by themselves. And really if you was to see with what ardent expectations some of the poor wretches watch the opportunity of looking out to sea, or the tears that are often shed upon the infants at the breast, you must have feelings that otherwise you could never have experiences of. (Hist. Rec. of N.S.W. Vol II)

Surgeon Charles Worgan gives a picture of the time:

> It is now so long since we have heard from home that our clothes are worn threadbare. We begin to think the mother country has entirely forsaken us. As for shoes, my stock has been exhausted these last six months and I have been obliged since that time to beg and borrow among the gentlemen, for no such article was to be bought. In this deplorable situation famine is staring us in the face. Two ounces of pork is the allowance of animal food for four and twenty hours, and happy is the man that can kill a rat or crow to make him a dainty meal. (Hist. Rec. of N.S.W. Vol II)

Not only shoes and clothes but fishing tackle was running out. This brought out the initiative in a convict who had been a ropemaker to start spinning lines from a bark of a tree that the natives used. Never forgetting the future, Phillip had the land prepared for the next sowing. Even in this darkest hour, he still had hope. While Surgeon White writes to a friend in London that if no relief came in seven months "the game would be up with us", Phillip writes, "We shall not starve. . ."

THE SECOND FLEET

The 3rd June was a wild, wet day but mid-afternoon brought great excitement. People ran and shouted and cried. A sail had been sighted. Everyone rushed to the shore and they saw a ship flying the British colours coming through the Heads. So anxious were they that they thought the ship was in danger. Three of them grabbed a small boat and rowed furiously. Tench, one of the three, is speaking to us again:

> The weather was wet and tempestuous but the body is delicate only when the soul is at ease. We pushed through wind and rain, the anxiety of our sensations every moment redoubling. At last we read the word London on her stern. 'Pull away, my lads! she's from old England! a few strokes more and we shall be aboard.'

Suddenly the hope was gone and the feeling of despair must have been worse than before their hopes were aroused. It was soon found out that on board there were 222 women convicts and no extra provisions for the colony. This was the *Lady Juliana*, the first of the second fleet. She brought the news that one thousand convicts were on their way as well as part of the garrison to relieve the present guard, that the *Gorgon*, carrying stores, would bring Major Grose and the rest of the N.S.W. Corps and – worst of all – she brought the news of the wreck of the *Guardian*. The *Guardian* was a ship fully laden with those things that Phillip had requested, with provisions for everybody to the value of £70,000 (abt $125,000), as well as much private property that had been sent to the officers by their families and friends. She also carried much livestock, which had been bought in Cape Town. Sir Joseph Banks had had the deck fitted out as a garden with hundreds of plants in it and he had sent one hundred and fifty fruit trees, some even bearing fruit. There were implements, clothing, blankets, bedding, medicines, sails, cordage and wine. There were 25 convicts who were farmers and artificers and seven men to act as supervisors. Much of the longed-for cargo went to the bottom of the sea when, on the 23rd December, the ship was wrecked. The story of the wreck of the *Guardian* is an epic in itself.

After twelve days' sailing from the Cape, an iceberg was sighted and, because of the need for water, the Captain, Lieutenant Edward Riou, made his way towards it and sent some men in boats to collect some ice. After they got it aboard, the ship, because of the direction of the winds and currents caused by the size of the iceberg, was drawn towards it and struck on part of it that was below the surface of the water. The force of the movement of the sea broke off the rudder. After throwing a lot overboard and doing much pumping, they became free of the iceberg, which then floated away. For the next two days they pumped furiously but, when the pumps broke down, their last hope of survival seemed to be the boats. They asked Riou to allow them to abandon ship. He fitted in with this request and then went and wrote an account of the wreck. A small number of men, including the ship's carpenter, a midshipman and the boatswain chose to stay with their captain while the others rowed off to what must have seemed like the last chance of survival. As it turned out, they were all drowned except those in one boat, which was rescued in fourteen days and taken to Cape Town. Those who stayed with the sinking ship, after nine weeks, reached Cape Town as a result of unexpected help of men and equipment lent to them by the captain of a passing Dutch ship. The story of the last struggle on the rudderless, water logged, bashed-up ship is told by the boatswain:

> After the boats left us we had two chances – either pump or sink. We could just get into the sail room. We got up

a new forecourse and stuck it full of oakum, and rags, and put it under the ship's bottom, this is called fothering the ship. We was in this terable situation for nine weeks before we got to the Cape of Good Hope. Sometimes our upper deck scuppers was under water outside, and the ship laying like a log on the water, and the sea breaking over her as if she was a rock in the sea. Sixteen foot of water was the common run for the nine weeks in the hold.(Hist. Rec. of N.S.W. Vol II)

Judging from a report of those who stayed with the wreck, the performance of the captain was magnificent all through this long-drawn-out trial and he must have had a wonderful relationship with those few who were with him to the end of it. Like so many seafaring men – many quite unknown – he allowed the sea – or rather, the dangers of life on the sea – to strengthen the already developing capacities for presence of mind, unselfishness and heroism.

MORE TROUBLE COMING

Now, Phillip had to face the fact that he had the responsibility of 222 more women. It was to be found that the majority became a burden to the colony. Two weeks later, the much awaited storeship arrived and the colony was put back onto full rations issued weekly. Bad weather still prevailed and shortly a ship was sighted but disappeared and was not seen for another two days. This ship carried some of the N.S.W. Corps which had been formed by volunteers to replace the existing guard. There were one hundred sick convicts put ashore, many others having died on the way. Two days later, after the arrival of two more ships, another two hundred sick convicts were landed. On these three ships many other convicts had died due to poor rations and overcrowding. Part of a letter from a convict who had arrived on the *Lady Juliana* gives a graphic picture of the terrible scene:

> Oh! if you had seen the shocking sight of the poor creatures that came out of the three ships it would make your

heart bleed; they were almost dead; very few could stand, and they were obliged to fling them as you would goods, and hoist them out of the ships, they were so feeble and they died ten to twelve a day when they first landed; but some of them are getting better . . . They were confined and had bad victuals and stinking water. The Governor was very angry and scolded the captain a great deal, and I heard, intended to write to London about it, for I heard him say it was murdering them.(Hist. Rec. of N.S.W. Vol II) (This letter is in the British Museum.)

As with so many evils, the cause was money – or rather the love of it – and the lack of love of the fellow man. The method of hiring transports was that the owner received £17 (about $30) per convict taken on board. As that covered the food, it meant that the less they had to eat and the greater the number of deaths the more money the owner would have. Phillip did report this tragedy and the owner was punished and the system of transportation was changed. Of the thousand convicts embarked, seven hundred and fifty were landed, of whom by the end of the next month, ninety more died and two hundred and twenty were still under medical care.

From his despatches, Phillip learnt that the N.S.W. Corps would consist of three hundred men, one hundred of which had already arrived. The existing guard, under the leadership of Major Ross, was to return to England unless they decided to take up one of the options open to them. They could stay and settle on the land or join the N.S.W. Corps. If they settled they would be given a grant of land and if they joined the Corps they would receive a bounty. If, after serving in the new guard, they decided to settle they would then be given a double grant of land.

Those convicts who were able to do any work were sent to Rose Hill and there the second settlement was established under Phillip's supervision. He planned wide streets, one leading from the place of landing to the foot of the hill where he was to build a house for himself. This street would be a mile (1.6km) long and two hundred feet (61m) wide. On each side of it, huts would be built to house ten men. Each allotment would be big enough for a small garden. All hands were put to clearing for building and cultivation. The following months were a time of expansion, which entailed − as well as the clearing − the building of huts and roads and making bricks.

In the Cove there was new life with the unloading of the ships, the building of new kilns, storehouses and roads. It was found, when unloading, that a lot of the provisions had been ruined by water getting into the hold. Phillip had wanted to send the *Lady Juliana* to Norfolk Island as soon as possible with provisions but, as she needed repairing before putting to sea again, it was late in July before two ships were sent to the Island. The situation there was desperate. The ship-wrecked crew of the *Sirius* were still there and there were the extra convicts.

THE STORY OF THE WHALE

It was in this month that an event took place that was to have a sequel. Four men were rowing from South Head to the Cove when the boat was attacked by a whale. Three were drowned and one got ashore to tell the tale. One of those drowned was James Ferguson, the seventeen-year-old son of the Lieutenant-Governor of Greenwich Hospital, the naval school where Phillip trained.

As July passed and August came, all eyes were often turned to the flagstaff on South Head. Watch was being kept continually for the arrival. of the *Gorgon*. Daniel Southwell, mate on the *Sirius* who was in charge of the watch station, was building a column as a landmark and it was on the 7th September that Phillip, as he had done with anything con-structed, went to inspect the work. On the way back, he was accompanied by Collins and Henry Waterhouse, midshipman from the *Sirius*. They were intercepted by a boat from Manly Cove with the message that Bennelong wanted to see him. John White and some others had landed at Manly Cove with the intention of doing some exploring. On landing, they had seen a crowd of natives feasting round a dead whale. White had seen Bennelong who expressed a wish to see the Governor. With a piece of whale for the Governor given by Bennelong, a boat was sent to intercept Phillip on his way back from South Head. The Governor, anxious to see Bennelong, changed his direction. At first, Phillip went towards the natives alone but was unable to recognize Bennelong. Collins and Waterhouse then accompanied him and they saw not only Bennelong but also Colbee. At first, the former was hesitant to come too close but in few minutes he was asking about all the people he knew at the settlement. Then Colbee approached and joined in the talk. After a time, another native, unknown to either of the others, came towards them and stood about thirty yards (27m) away. Phillip, in his usual way, held out his arm, beckoning him to come closer but the native, thinking he was going to capture him, stood back and fixed his spear. Thinking it safer to advance than retreat, Phillip stepped towards the native who then stepped back and threw the spear with such force that the barb went through his shoulder and came out at the back. As the spear was about ten feet in length, it continually struck the ground in front of him as he moved towards the boat. Waterhouse tried to break it without success the first time and it was only after further effort that it was broken. The distance from the scene of this happening to medical help was about five miles and necessitated passing the Heads. The rowers, alarmed at the amount of blood coming from the wound, made the distance in under two hours.

The spear head was removed on return and it was found that the wound was not as serious as it could have been. In ten days, he was getting about again. There was no retaliation and Phillip realized that the native could reasonably have thought that he was going to be captured. The whole episode, in the end, brought about a better relationship between the natives and the newcomers.

After the two years with the convicts of the first fleet, some law and order had been achieved amongst those who were capable of co-operation but now the Governor was faced with the new batch. Crime increased again and, with so much shipping about, attempts to escape by sea occurred.

BENNELONG RETURNS

It was not till October that Bennelong came and met the Governor again. This was repeated even to the extent of bringing other natives with him. He persuaded Phillip to build them a hut like the white man's on the eastern point of the Cove.

The return of the *Supply* from Batavia eased the situation slightly. The hired Dutch ship with the rest of the provisions was on its way but did not arrive till December.

Building was continuing. A vein of clay was found at Rose Hill which led to the making of bricks there but the settlements were about to suffer their first drought. The crops were not thriving and fire became a danger.

Rose Hill was going ahead with about two hundred acres (80 hectares) having been cleared for cultivation. The main street had been started, a brick storehouse, a house for the Governor and the first story of a barracks had been built as well as a barn, a granary and a blacksmith's shop. A temporary hospital had been put up also.

The Sydney scene had changed. Cultivation had almost ceased and the government farm had been abandoned. Instead, much building was taking place. A large brick storehouse and a hospital and permanent barracks were to be started soon. This increase of work was brought about by the fact that the convicts now had supervision.

1791

On the 22nd January, the *Supply* was sent to Norfolk Island to bring Hunter and the men of the *Sirius* back to Port Jackson. On the 26th, the first Anniversary Day was celebrated. Shortly after, Henry Dodd, who had been such a help at Rose Hill, died. His death was hastened by the fact that he got from his sickbed to chase after convicts robbing his garden. He searched for them for hours, after which he had a relapse and died.

HUNTER LEAVES

The heat was worse than it had ever been. Tench makes the statement that he thought the "winds must blow off immense deserts". Water became scarce and the temperature soared to 105° (40.6C). The *Supply* returned in February with Hunter and the men. They stayed in the military barracks and hospital until the Dutch hired ship was able to take them on board for their return trip to England. Ten of the crew and two marines stayed and the others who left at the end of March did not arrive in England until April 1792 after a terrible voyage.

RUSE SUCCESSFUL

Because of so many escapes and attempts to escape, Phillip had to put guards over all small boats. It was again a hard time as it had been at this time of the year since they arrived. Rations had to be reduced again and water was short. The one bit of good news was from Rose Hill. James Ruse, who proved himself worthy of Phillip's trust in him, reported that he could now give up drawing on the stores, that he was self-sufficient. This must have meant both relief and joy to Phillip.

FURTHER EXPLORATION

At this time, Phillip asked for relief to go to England for medical attention and then return. He had, for about two years, never been free of the pain in his side. In spite of his state of health he went on yet another journey of exploration. More people meant more land was needed and he was ready to go to find some and he had still to solve the problem about the two rivers. Were they one and the same?

It was a big party that set out with twenty-one altogether including two natives. Equipped for ten days, they left on the 11th April from Rose Hill. The natives were helpful but not in the way it had been imagined they would be. They did not know the area but they did help with contact with other natives. Many days of hard travelling were experienced, following

VIEW OF PART OF THE TOWN OF PARRAMATTA, IN NEW SOUTH WALES
Drawn by J. Eyre. Engraved by P. Slaeger. Published 1812. By kind permission of The National Library of Australia, Canberra

rivers and crossing creeks but they were no nearer to solving the problem about the rivers and so, after ten days, they returned to Rose Hill. It was not until Tench and Dawes were sent again in another effort to find out that no doubt was left about the rivers being one.

LAND GRANTS

Phillip's administrative work had increased with the increase of numbers and from time to time he made land grants to people who became eligible for settling. The ground had become so hard that it was impossible to do the work of preparation for the next sowing with the people showing the effects of famine again. Just as casks were being sunk into the ground to let water seep into them, the rain came – enough to get the sowing done for the next year.

The *Supply* on her return trip had been buffeted about so much that she was overdue and so badly damaged that she was out of action for some time.

This year, for the first time, the King's birthday was celebrated at Rose Hill. It was on this day that the Governor renamed the town Parramatta after the natives' word meaning "where eels sit down". Phillip also made some concessions to those convicts who were serving sentence for thieving and, that very night, six men raided his garden and assaulted the watchman.

THE THIRD FLEET

It was in July of that year that ships started to arrive, bringing more convicts. The first brought clothing, a few provisions and 140 women convicts, six children and a free woman. With the news that Phillip Gidley King was in England, came the other news that 2050 convicts were on their way! Not only that but there was a plan to send regular shipments of convicts twice a year. Because of the condition of the provisions, Collins says, "It was so worm-eaten that this meant practically nothing. . . Of 60 lbs of meat issued in one to two messes, 40 lbs was bone, and the remainder . . . was almost too far advanced in putrefaction for even hunger to get down."

SYDNEY FROM THE EAST SIDE OF THE COVE
John Eyre, 1811. By kind permission of the Mitchell Library, Sydney

Still there were the problems of thieving and escaping and it became necessary to make all trading with convicts illegal. It was in August that another ship came in with 205 more convicts, with provisions for nine months. This eased the situation. Twenty-five had died on the way and a further twenty were sick on arrival. The ship itself was in such a state that Phillip could not send it on to Norfolk Island as he had intended: He sent another ship with a further thirty-two convicts and eleven of the N.S.W. Corps. A couple of weeks later, the *Atlantic* arrived with 220 men convicts, mostly in good health. Phillip sent this ship and her cargo and people to Norfolk Island.

Full rations came in again at the end of August. The problem now was what to do with so many convicts. Some went to Parramatta but the rest remained in Sydney. A week later, yet another ship arrived with 181 convicts in good health and more members of the N.S.W Corps. As the number of possible settlers was increasing, Parramatta spread out to Toongabbie and Prospect.

TURNING POINT

This month saw the arrival of the long-awaited *Gorgon*. Phillip was to get some help, at last, for on board were Lieutenant King and his wife, a Surveyor-General for Norfolk Island, a superintendent of convicts, a chaplain for the N.S.W. Corps, provisions for nine hundred for six months, livestock, 200 fruit trees and a lot of garden seed. The Governor's public seal, which should have come with the First Fleet, was also on board.

The arrival of this ship was a turning point, for the settlement was given a new impetus but, only six days later, two more ships arrived to cause more strain. The Home Government had not yet learnt the necessity for supervision on transport ships. Not only was it found that the convicts were ill-treated on these ships but also that the ship had brought a lot of private cargo instead of the things that were desperately needed in the colony. Phillip hated the fact that tonnage being paid for by the Government had been used for private enterprise and wrote the following to Lord Grenville:

EARLY GOVERNMENT HOUSE
From *The Picturesque Atlas of Australasia, 1886*

Your Lordship will readily conceive how much consequence it would have been to the settlement had two or three hundred tons of limestone been sent out, and which might have been done, if those ships found it necessary to bring out so much shingle ballast; for the limestone might with little trouble have been changed to the stone of this country.

MORE SHIPPING

Two more ships arrived bringing a further 270 men and 23 women convicts all in a bad state. Some of them were the first to come from Ireland.

October saw three more ships anchoring in the harbour, all within three days. They brought a further 643 men and six women convicts, four free women and some children.

After this sudden increase of mouths to be fed, Phillip sent the *Atlantic* to Calcutta for more provisions. In reporting this move, he wrote the following to Lord Grenville:

> When the provisions brought out with the convicts, and what was received of the *Guardian's* cargo, and the surplus of the *Gorgon's* provisions were added to what we have in the colony it only gave us five months' flour, ten months' beef and pork, twelve days' pease and twenty-three days' oatmeal.

It was in November of this fourth year that he made the decision to request permission to resign from the Governorship of the colony. There was a double purpose in this request. One purpose was to interview the authorities himself to try to get a better direction for the further work to be done and the other was to find out whether there was still a chance for him to recover from his illness sufficiently to be able to return to the colony if that were requested of him. In this letter to the Home Office, he pointed out that, as far as the necessities of life were concerned, he was now at last certain that the colony could be independent but it appears that he was still anxious that the colony should achieve something more than production of the barest necessities.

In December, there was the experience of the departure of all the ships, including the *Gorgon*. They took back to England many of his responsible officers and the marines whose term was expired. Some did choose to remain and settle. Before Christmas, the rations were reduced again. Even on Christmas Day, the store was robbed and 22 gallons (100 litres) of spirits stolen. Rations were again issued daily and the convicts were unsettled about that. It was on the last day of the year that the first rumblings of revolt occurred. Convicts assembled in front of Government House at Parramatta and requested that their rations be served weekly as usual. Phillip dismissed them without granting their request. What he did was to threaten to make an example of the ringleaders if they did not promise to be more co-operative.

During this year of 1791, the population of the colony reached 4059 people. There were 1259 in Sydney, 1628 in Parramatta and 1172 at Norfolk Island.

1792

If Phillip dreaded anything, he must have dreaded the approaching year, as it had become obvious that there would be times of harvest and thieving; times of serious shortage of food; then the struggle against weakness, which meant a further slowing up of the work, specially the work of preparing for the following sowing; then the arrival of more ships and the assimilation of the strangers and then back to harvest and thieving again. It must have been obvious to Phillip that, although this pattern of events was likely to repeat itself, things would in a way be very different. There would be expansion in civil life as well as in commercial life. Phillip could not work to any set of governmental rules. He had to govern this country as circumstances occurred and changed. The needs of the colony governed the Governor. Another way of saying this is that the Governor was always so alert as to be able to act quickly on his own observation of the ever-changing circumstances.

TRADING BEGINS

Crime still occupied much attention. Not only food but also clothes and hospital needs were being stolen. Up till now, the thieving had been carried out by individuals but now it was plotted and carried out by gangs. One such plot was made to capture the storehouse! Although it was stopped, the need arose for more laws, such as the one forbidding convicts to assemble in order to make a complaint and the one stating that anyone disturbing sleep or rest-time would be arrested. On the other hand, more and more settlers were helping the more helpless convicts to behave in a better way. Tracts of land on the north side of the harbour were given to those marines who decided against returning home and Phillip started up private trade. This meant that people could sell their grain or anything else amongst the other settlers and that what was not sold would be bought by the Government at a fair price. This was the beginning of regular legal trade. Prior to this, the masters of the ships had set up markets, when in port, for their own gains and without permission but now trade was part of the life of the colony. In April, this idea was expanded and a market was set up at Parramatta which allowed convicts to trade under strict regulations.

A NEW LIEUTENANT-GOVERNOR

Early in February, another ship arrived bringing Major Grose, who was the next Lieutenant-Governor and Commander of the N.S.W. Corps. On the same ship, came more than 300 convicts and ten months' supply of salt meat! Though encouraging private trade amongst the settlers, Phillip had to complain to the politicians again about the way this ship had a big part of its stowage space taken up with goods for trade by the master and very little of it for goods urgently needed by all. His letter of complaint goes on to say:

> It is not, sir, to reflect on the person who commanded the *Pitt* that I make this observation, but from feeling the obligation of pointing a circumstance which may prevent a

similar evil, the effects of which are at this moment severely felt in the colony.

His letter is full of restraint seeing that he had to witness "luxuries such as ribbons and fancy hats taking up space in the ships where axes and cooking pots could have been."

At this time there was a further worry. The *Atlantic*, which had been sent to Bengal for provisions, had not returned and he feared for its safety. In case it had been wrecked, he sent another ship giving the captain a duplicate order and instructions that, if he heard it had been, to bring the order back as soon as possible.

It was on the 17th February that Major Grose's commission was read by the Judge-Advocate, who had remained in the colony. The fact that he remained was a great relief to Phillip. The time of the year was at hand when the settlement was again to face yet another time of possible starvation. In his despatches, Phillip was still asking for superintendents and now he was asking for ships to replace the *Sirius* and the *Supply*. Ships that were supposed to have left England about the previous September had not arrived and Phillip had no certainty that they had been sent. Amazingly, he still continued to believe in the future of this colony and went on planning the town that was to rise on the shores of Sydney Cove.

STARVATION THREATENS AGAIN

Reservoirs were built and, although by June the population of N.S.W. was in a state of general weakness, the overall situation was heading for the better. There was the threat of still further reduction of food, as there was only enough flour in store for one month and enough salted meat for two months. Although things were certainly looking black at the time, the future held more hope because enough ground had been cleared to yield enough wheat for a year. There still was the question as to whether enough people would have enough strength to do the vital sowing.

SOME RELIEF

The *Atlantic* brought some relief when it eventually returned at the end of June and further relief came a month later when another ship arrived with enough flour for eight months. It was from this ship that Phillip received a despatch containing the following:

> It will, however, be a satisfaction to you to know that considering the inconveniences with which you have had to struggle, they are perfectly satisfied that everything has been done by you which could under the circumstances, be reasonably expected.

The next three months were a time of recovery and expansion. The rains came and, in the middle of September, the *Atlantic* sailed with one-third of the new stock of provisions for Norfolk Island. One ship moved out of the Cove and anchored off Bradley's Head and prepared, as it was thought, for sailing to New Zealand. However, at the beginning of October, Phillip received a letter from Major Grose informing him that the members of the N.S.W. Corps had hired the ship to go, instead, to the Cape to get private stores for themselves. Phillip saw the action as one that could lead to private profit for a section of the population which could then easily become the dominating class at the expense of those who were more interested in the venture as a whole than in their own personal gain. He did suggest that, in future, transport owners be asked to call at the Cape and take on board some commodities and that, when ships went to Calcutta, officers could send private orders.

Further despatches left on the transport that sailed in October. From these we can see that he never gave up pleading for the good of the colony:

> It has, sir, been my fate to point out wants from year to year; it has been a duty the severest I have ever experienced. Did those wants only respect myself or a few individuals I should be silent; but there are numbers who bear

them badly; nor has the colony suffered more from wanting what we have not received than from the supplies we have received not arriving in time.

HIS RESIGNATION

He also wrote again about himself and his situation:

> I believe my returning to England will be the greatest service I can render this colony, independent of any other consideration, for it will put it in my power to shew what may and what may not be expected from it.

Phillip had sent King for the purpose of letting the Home Office know these things but he was not successful in pressing the point.

It was also in October that another of the expected ships arrived, bringing 289 men and 49 women convicts, a free-farmer, a master-miller and a master-carpenter.

As conditions on the transports were still far from satisfactory, Phillip wrote again saying that he thought the ships were too crowded. From this latest arrival he heard that a ship from America carrying all sorts of things was on its way and he had a reply from the Home Office to his resignation which still left him in doubt as to whether his resignation had been accepted. As his health was rapidly getting worse, he pleaded again for some assurance one way or the other. He, of course, did not say so but it is obvious now that, apart from health considerations, he needed to be in England for the sake of the settlement.

LAST FEW WEEKS

The healthy convicts who came on the previous ship were transferred straight to Parramatta, without even putting foot in Sydney. Collins gives the reason:

> . . . which town from the circumstances of its being the only place where shipping anchored, possessed all the evils and allurements of a seaport of some standing.

Thieving continued and some daring robberies took place, the master of the *Royal Admiral* set up a market and there was also an issue of clothing during October. It was at the end of this month that Phillip made public the fact that he was returning to England. This was quite unexpected and in some circles caused quite a shock. He was to return on the *Atlantic*.

Early in November, the American ship arrived laden with commodities. Phillip purchased beef, pitch and tar and the rest was bought up by the community.

The arrival of another ship brought a few more disappointments. It was to have brought fifty Quaker families but they had decided to go somewhere else; eight of the ten artisans had escaped; the ship had sprung a leak during a stormy journey and part of the provisions were ruined and the iron pots that had at last been sent had nearly all been broken by the buffeting. Nevertheless, the arrival of this ship meant that rations were increased for the time.

The time for the hot weather had come and another warning was given. After having harvested the wheat crop at Toongabbie, a bush-fire swept through the stubble. It was brought home to everybody that, if it had happened before harvesting, they would have faced a major setback. Phillip gave another order – most likely his last – that fire-breaks were to be made and maintained around cultivated areas. His last official engagement was the opening of Parramatta Hospital.

At 6 p.m. on the 10th December, he boarded the *Atlantic* after a farewell given, with full honours, by the N.S.W. Corps. With him, he took two time-expired convicts and two native people, Bennelong and Yemmerrawannie.

BACK IN ENGLAND

Although he received some relief from his illness, Phillip resigned in 1793, as he was given no hope of returning to Sydney Cove. Yet, his task was by no means completed. One of the most important and difficult parts of his work would have been the counteracting of the misrepresentations of both the country and of himself. This misrepresentation must, all the time, have been interfering with his relationship with the authorities. It must have taken all his tact and perseverance to influence the Government to look with favour on the settlement. The intensity of his interest in it must have made him strain every nerve to bring about what he had always longed for – the introducing of competent, helpful people to the country of his heart. This had been hindered not only by depressing accounts written by some marine and civil officers but also by the fact that people could go to overseas places that were closer to home and better known. It is quite possible that the authorities were not anxious to see Phillip, knowing that he would go on fighting for the rights and needs of the people so easily forgotten because they were so far away. He was the only one who could continue the work that he had begun and some wonderful people did start to go out as free settlers. Not long after resigning from his governorship, he remarried – his first wife having died.

His Portuguese associates had recognized that ill health made no difference to the enthusiasm with which he threw himself into work, so it is not surprising that, while his health must have become very precarious, we hear that he returned to the British Navy in 1796. After being at sea for two years and when France was again threatening to invade Britain, Phillip was called upon again to help with the defence of Britain. All fishing boats around the east coast of England and all who knew something about the sea were mobilised. In 1798, he was put in charge of reorganizing part of this but the next year he was made commander and organizer of what became known as the *Sea Defensibles*. He carried out this task till 1805, then he retired and lived in Bath for his remaining year. From the fact that it was within a year of his retirement that he had a severe stroke –paralysing the right side of the body – it is easy to see that he had been coping with a deterioration of health for many years.

The eight years of enforced physical inactivity must have been a painful experience. He had been essentially a practical man always ready to spring into action. The whole course of his life points to his ability to accept fully whatever difficulties life would bring. The fact that he was mentally active and interested in life till the end suggests that he still would have been doing all he could to influence people who could help the colony to take an interest in it.

On the 31st August 1814, the magnificent fund of health he must have inherited was all spent. He died in obscurity – not casting even a ripple on the pond of public opinion. In spite of the fact that he had risen through the ranks of the Royal Navy to become an Admiral, there were no last honours and only a few in attendance as the body was taken through the quiet lanes to the village church. There was no publicity, no public recognition in England or Australia and no descendants to keep alive the memory of his illustrious name and his history-making work. He went out as quietly and modestly as he came into that life of self-denial, lived out for the sake of humanity.

AFTERTHOUGHTS

What king had had to make a perilous sea journey of about thirteen thousand miles (21,000km), then step onto land and, the very·same day, start to rule over a completely unknown situation? George Mackaness points out that besides all the rest "he had to establish the machinery of a civil government". What king had had to live at such close quarters with his subjects – available to anybody day or night? What king had had to suffer the anguish of having to witness executions, knowing that he had the power to call them off but also knowing that, if he did too much of that, he would be guilty of encouraging crime and bringing on wholesale starvation and increasing chaos? What king or prison governor had had to live separated only by walls of canvas from criminals who could be expected to hate him who had the power of life and death over them?

Phillip was, of course, not a king. However, he did have a kingly nature as a result of an unusual degree of mastery over his thoughts and feelings and, therefore, over his actions. Those who were capable of respect where respect is due respected him and accepted his authority. In spite of having this in his favour, he was not carried away by it. This becomes obvious when it is noticed that he was in the process of making himself into a servant. He was an uncomplaining, undemanding person and yet he did not hesitate to make strong complaints when he saw injustice that could be stopped. For example, there was his strong complaint to the Government about the cruelty to all aboard some of the convict ships – his complaint being against the system that allowed greedy men to make money out of the neglect of those in their charge. Because he was undemanding for himself, he was able to keep himself free for any demands that would be put upon him by his work. Yet he did demand that people at the Cove respect each others' need for food. He was ready to demand that the white people respect the natives' right to their own belongings and their own moral code and he was determined to learn about them and to give severe punishment to the white people who interfered with them.

In so many ways, he gives the impression of balance. Surrounded by depression mounting often to despair, surrounded by dishonesty and lack of understanding of his purposes, Phillip maintained the steadiness of hope and the drive of purpose and the gentleness of increasing forbearance. He gives, too, the impression of harmony, which was able to stand up to incredible disharmony in his surroundings. This harmony seems to be connected with his unbiased sort of attitude to people.

In the life of Arthur Phillip, we have a picture that makes it obvious that the destiny of an individual is woven in with the destiny of the whole of mankind. This life becomes even more interesting when studied with the past and the future in mind. For instance, it throws light on the intriguing way in which his personal life was woven into his public life in such mellow colours that one hardly notices it. The study throws light on the way the timing of great and small happenings seemed to have served his main purpose.

His way of government formed the foundation for the continuing government of the country. Phillip was able, by foresight and flexibility, to bring about changes without making fixed reforms. As thoughts have more influence than is generally realized, the strength, soundness and stability of his thinking capacity seem to give justification for the suggestion, put forward in the Introduction, that his influence – if he were well known – could have an effect on the country's development that would be stronger than the influence of those amongst the convicts who did bring in degrading influences. Through suffering, degrading influences could gradually work themselves out and the thought-filled purposes that were at work in the soul of Arthur Phillip could gradually work themselves in.

What was it in this man that made it possible for him to carry out such a mighty task in a state of such physical weakness and ill health? What was it in him that would not allow pain, sorrow, terrible conditions and mighty opposition to prevent the nation of his vision from arising, surviving and developing?

What makes a city great? Huge piles of stone
Heaped heavenward? Vast multitudes who dwell
Within wide circling walls? Palace and throne
And riches past the count of man to tell,
And wide domain? Nay, these the empty husk!
True glory dwells where glorious deeds are done,
Where great men rise whose names athwart the dusk
Of misty centuries gleam like the sun!
In Athens, Sparta, Florence, t'was the soul
That was the city's bright immortal part,
The splendor of the spirit was their goal,
Their jewel the unconquerable heart!
So may the city that I love be great
Till every stone shall be articulate.

William Dudley F. Foulke

His life was gentle, and the elements
So mixed in him, that nature might stand up
And say to all the world, This was a man!

Shakespeare

TITLES BY THE SAME AUTHOR

James Cook*
Dear Humanity*
Enduring Deeds†
Alternative Thinking
The Unknown Drug*
Towards Social Health
For Your Spare Moment*
For Your Spare Half-Hour*
Twentieth Century Question*
Towards Self Development*
Men in the Making (Vols. 1 & 2)
*Available on cassette
†Part of this book available on cassette

Copies of the books listed above should be readily available from your local bookshop or library. Should you experience difficulty in obtaining any of the titles you may be order direct from the publisher. A free catalogue will be sent on request.

MOVEMENT PUBLICATIONS
10 Argyle Place, Millers Point, N.S.W. 2000, Australia
Telephone: 27 7029